T0128394

FINDING CHRIST IN THE BOOK OF REVELATION

ADULT WORKBOOK FOR CHRISTIAN DISCIPLESHIP

ARLAND DAVID POMERINKE

WestBow Press books may be ordered through booksellers or by contacting:

WestBow Press
A Division of Thomas Nelson & Zondervan
1663 Liberty Drive
Bloomington, IN 47403
www.westbowpress.com
1 (866) 928-1240

Photographer: Katherine Ketcham

All Scripture quotations are taken from the King James Version.

ISBN: 978-1-9736-7848-9 (sc)
ISBN: 978-1-9736-7847-2 (e)

Library of Congress Control Number: 2019917277

Print information available on the last page.

WestBow Press rev. date: 11/27/2019

Behold, I stand at the door, and knock: if any man hear my voice, and open the door, I will come in to him, and will sup with him, and he with me. To him that overcometh will I grant to sit with me in my throne, even as I also overcame, and am set down with my Father in his throne. He that hath an ear, let him hear what the Spirit saith unto the churches. Revelation 3:20-22 (KJV)

Dedication:
To Harriet Garland and Carrol Williams, and to all those whom I love who have gone before to be with Christ.

Contents

Acknowledgements

I want to say thanks to my mom and sisters, to my wonderful wife Melinda, and to my children; I cannot imagine life without you. To the many friends and family members who have stood by me throughout my life, I know the many hours you spent supporting me over many years was a sacrifice and I love you for this. I also acknowledge my religion professors from college, my pastors, and my closest mentors of the faith. Those who spent many hours debating doctrine and spirituality with me. You caused a desire for God to rise in me and I appreciate you. Finally, to all of my spiritual allies I say, you were God's design and plan to keep me accountable throughout my life and I will never be able to thank you enough for your guidance.

A.D. Pomerinke ∝

Introduction to Revelation Study

Throughout my many years working with small groups and Sunday School classes I have participated in many studies in the book of Revelation. Now, when you love to study God's Word, and when you love to discuss controversial topics like religion, politics and eschatology, that's when you decide your next project should be to write a discipleship study for the book of Revelation! Although I felt God was leading me to write this study, my first thought was that I'm just not qualified, it would be a difficult task that would take months of research and translation, and I was intimidated by the entire process. In the end, I had to turn to my spiritual allies for direction and encouragement to continue. My hope for this workbook is to offer adult Christians, both individuals and groups, the opportunity to complete a study of the book of Revelation that has spiritual relevance in their lives. In order to reach this goal, I came to understand that within the study of eschatology there are many influences, personal thoughts, doctrines, and even spiritual biases or preconceived ideas that form a person's expectations of who they believe God is and how one should view the end times prophesies. While studying and discussing this topic, the most common questions that I was asked was if I support the pre-tribulation, mid-tribulation, or post-tribulation theology? Many of my friends and family members even asked me to own my position on when and if I feel the rapture will happen. Pastors sometimes would start our discussion with these types of questions, and I learned quickly that this was usually not an open-ended question, but it was literally an invitation to a debate. I realize that many have already spent time in study, reinforcing their point of view, and that many Christians have already discussed end of days doctrines to the point that they have built an unshakable understanding of just how all of the end times will go down. There was, however, one thing I found universally common with most persons interested in eschatology, it was that within these dedicated disciples of Christ, within their preconceived doctrines and biases, was a true desire to find Christ in Revelation, and it is to that end that this study is offered.

This is not a study designed to turn anyone away from their doctrine or beliefs, but rather it is a method that groups, and individuals, can use to explore the call from God to find Christ in Revelation. To apply the messages of salvation, redemption, justification and sanctification to an evangelical understanding of the call that still exists within the church to fulfill the Great Commission. This is my desire for this study, and it is with this purpose I ask you to pray for the Holy Spirit to guide you. Ask God to release you from closed-mindedness and to help you accept His guidance in this effort. Also, ask God to remind you of your connection to all other believers, who are also, in humility, seeking the knowledge of God. The one universal goal we all as Christians can agree upon is that we want to serve God in all that we do. This journey of learning obedience and understanding can be revealed and fulfilled during the coming months if you allow the Holy Spirit to lead you.

This study is prepared for groups or individuals and is set up to have one session a week. Some try to cover two sessions a week and this is possible. I can say from experience that anyone can jump into this study at any point and still be blessed from the session curriculums. God bless you all in your efforts to understand Christ and the Kingdom of God in a greater way. Until the end of the age, keep serving God!

A.D. Pomerinke

Prep-Session with Background Information,

THIS SHOULD BE THE READING AND DISCUSSION TO OPEN YOUR STUDY ON REVELATION

Christian tradition holds that Revelation was written by John the Beloved, a disciple of Jesus and an apostle and patriarch of the early church. This letter entitled Revelation, which means path to truth, was defined by John as a vision and message from Jesus Christ. It was delivered somewhere close to 60 years after the death, resurrection, and ascension of Jesus. This means that it was absolutely God's will for John to survive those long years under the tyranny of persecution he and his fellow Christians had encountered while working to fulfill God's plan for the church. At the time of this vision John was the last of the original twelve disciples, as far as we know. The other eleven were already passed on from this Earth, and it is probable that John himself was longingly awaiting his own departure unto God. They had all given everything for Christ, except for John; he had not yet given his life for the Gospel. Remember that Jesus had foretold of John's longevity after His resurrection as He spent those last few days with His disciples. That encounter in John 21 tells us of a future purpose from God for John to be the one to deliver this apocalyptic message to the church.

The location where John was writing is identified as being on a small island, near the west coast of modern-day Turkey, called Patmos. This island still exists today in the area known as Asia Minor. Christian tradition holds two main views of why John was on this island. The first and more supported tradition was that John was exiled for preaching the Good News of the Messiah, which the early church called The Way. This exile for the faith came under the direction of Roman Emperor Titus Flavious Domitianus, and is thought to have happened on or around 95 AC. Domitianus was a contemporary of Caesar Nero who was the initiator of the tyrannical and satanic hatred that Rome had towards the Christian Church. The second view, which has fewer followers, is that John made regular stops in this isolated place to retreat, to recover from the strains of mission work, and to avoid the conflicts which raged over this controversial religion. This background could have led John to take a break and renew himself. However, since history records that there was a Roman outpost on this island, most believe that John was probably incarcerated there and under watch when he wrote of this encounter with his Lord. In this vision, John sets about writing seven letters to the seven churches in Asia Minor, as he was commanded to do by Christ. These letters are still relevant for the church today, as all Cristian's are asked to read and study these messages.

Definitions:

allegory (Wikipedia, https://en.wikipedia.org/wiki/Allegory, 2018): As a literary device, an allegory is a metaphor in which a character, place or event is used to deliver a broader message about real-world issues and occurrences.

symbolism (Merriam-Webster Dictionary, https://www.merriam-webster.com/help/citing-the-dictionary, 2018): The practice of representing things by symbols, or of investing things with a symbolic meaning or character; the use of any of certain special figures or marks of identification to signify a religious message or divine being, as in the cross for Christ and the Christian faith or the symbol of the fish, <><, for the early church.

literal (the free dictionary, <a href="https://www.thefreedictionary.com/literalizing">literalizing</a>): Conforming or limited to the simplest, nonfigurative, or most obvious meaning of a word or words; A word taken at verbatim i.e. *a literal translation; without* exaggeration, metaphor, or embellishment; factual.

eschatology (Merriam-Webster Dictionary, https://www.merriam-webster.com/help/citing-the-dictionary, 2018): A branch of theology concerned with the final events in the history of the world or of humankind; a belief concerning death, the end of the world, or the ultimate destiny of humankind, specifically any of various Christian doctrines concerning the Second Coming, the resurrection of the dead, or the Last Judgment.

Reflections

During my study for this workbook I have read many different opinions on whether we should view the book of Revelation in a literal sense or view it as more of a complex system of allegories and symbols. Modern thought and trends that oppose Christianity have labeled this type of writing as rhetorical and fictitious in nature. We can see the advantage of using allegory and symbols to make sense of this story, especially from John's standpoint, but to those of faith we do not accept that any of this vision is a fictitious story.

I believe that the Apostle John used every literary tool he could to describe and explain things that he did not fully understand himself. And just as it is with many who study eschatology today, whose primary goal is to make sense of what is read, this was the same for John. I am sure that, while trying to make sense of Revelation, from a human standpoint, the visions John saw seemed impossible to fathom. Just what Jesus was relaying must have been very puzzling for John at times, as it can be for us today. The gift of this type of study is that the meanings hidden within Revelation can be better explained and understood within the modern realities of our world today. The literary styles used by John must have seemed far-fetched and supernatural to many minds of that day. However, we can find validity and proof of God's hand on this work by seeing the modern interpretation of these events. This miracle of modern knowledge has only reinforced, in a greater way, that God's Word should include Revelation as scripture and that it is even more valid in our modern understanding than it must have seemed in the time that it was written. So, to convey this message in allegory, symbolism, and rhetoric was God's plan, and it was a plan that would embrace the whole of church history.

As you read through these chapters and discuss their meaning you must remember that, while these symbols allow us to better understand the coming events in time, we are still discussing real people, nations, and events that will take place. The topics can be intimidating and cause fear unless the focus is on the work of grace found in knowing Christ even in turmoil and evil times. Jesus said, "I am the Alpha and the Omega, the First and the Last, what you see, write in a book and send it to the seven churches which are in Asia, to Ephesus, to Smyrna, to Pergamos, to Thyatira, to Sardis, to Philadelphia, and to Laodicea." (Revelation 1:11). This command that John was given, to share this message in allegories and symbols, applies even to the church today, to you and to me. This directive to consider the events which have taken place, are taking place, or will take place are a step of obedience for the Christian. Just as He used parables in His teachings, Jesus now is using these allegories and symbols, not unlike parables, to share the infinite wisdom of God in a sometimes-figurative way while also in a very real way.

The Leading of the Holy Spirit is the Key to Success

It is important to remember that, just as Jesus shared this revelation with John while he was in the Spirit, He also will send the Holy Spirit to reveal its meaning and nature to us today. As we walk by the Spirit of God in this pursuit for knowledge and understanding, we can truly come to understand just what God is doing even if we cannot understand how he will do it. Jesus gave John many symbols to ponder, but John was not to consider them and try to record what he was thinking they might mean; he simply recorded what he saw and heard and left the interpretation up to the reader by the leading of the Holy Spirit. In some cases, Jesus shares the meaning of the symbols we read about; he explained things to John, and to the future readers. As mentioned before, some of these symbols are more easily understood today than they were when John received this vision, and we know that these events will involve real people, all the nations of the world, and all the cultures on this Earth. It will include disasters and hardships unlike any the world has seen, and creatures that are beyond our imagination, as if we will be living in a real-life science fiction movie.

Because of this, I again invite your group to pray at the start of each session, seeking the Holy Spirit's leading in this study. Make sure to apply the grace that God has given you to others as you seek knowledge and understanding. Pray for God to allow you to accept that others have an opinion that is valid to them and to the message we are sharing. Let us remember that with eschatological discussion fear can rise, and that mandates a good understanding of God's love and grace to direct our trust of His goodness to us. Be prepared to encourage your brothers and sisters in Christ, and remember we need to find Christ in this study.

Preparation Session Questions:

Discuss the definitions and commentary above. As a group, set in your minds what your perspective should be while you study Revelation. Instead of focusing on the accuracy of interpreting events and times, focus on what Christ has done, is doing, and will do in the church and in the hearts of the saints.

1. What thoughts are you having as you prepare for this study?
2. As a group, each share how you plan to "find Christ" in this study.
3. What is your commitment level to following the weekly assignments? Share truthfully how much time you can spend on this.
4. Discuss your understanding of the end times doctrines.
5. What possibly can we gain by studying Revelations?
6. What are your personal goals for this study?
7. What are your corporate goals for this study?

Instructions to prepare for each session:

This study is designed to start each session with the leader giving an introduction before the group.

1. This introduction should include a group prayer for guidance.
2. Then the reading of the scripture assigned to that week's study.
3. A review of the word studies and commentary that participants have read through before the session.
4. Larger groups then split into table groups and hold a 30- to 45-minute discussion of the session.
5. These groups can discuss the questions and then the participants' own journal entries to complete the small group time.
6. After this the large group will reconvene and the leader can discuss the questions in a large group situation.
7. One hour to 90 minutes should be allowed for each session.

In each study there is opportunity for those who have kept a journal of their own comments and questions to share these with their group. Each person should know that their reflections and questions are relevant.

I do encourage you to follow the guidelines for this study, and to complete the preparation work each week, as over the coming months it will help all to develop a daily devotional lifestyle. The personal study during the week is designed to use repetition and journaling to help you come to understand Revelation in a deeper way.

Each group member should remember to ask friends and family to join the study, as even after it has begun persons can still be blessed by participating in the discussions. Remember that each study is also designed to be used as an individual lesson.

Assignment for Session 1:

- Set a plan to read Revelation chapter one every day for a week leading up to session 1.
- Complete session one by reading the workbook page and answering the questions in your personal journal or the note pages in this workbook, where you can also record any thoughts and questions you have. You will be able to share your thoughts and questions in session one.

Session 1

FINDING CHRIST IN REVELATION

Revelation 1:1-3 (KJV)

JOHN THE APOSTLE'S INTRODUCTION

(1) The **Revelation** of Jesus Christ, which God gave unto him, to shew unto his servants things which must shortly come to pass; and he sent and signified it by his angel unto his servant John: **(2)** Who bare record of the word of God, and of the **testimony** of Jesus Christ, and of all things that he saw. **(3) Blessed** is he that **readeth**, and they that **hear** the words of this prophecy, and keep those things which are written therein: for the time is at hand.

Revelation (GRK: ἀποκάλυψις / ap-ok-al'-oop-sis): A disclosure of truth; an instruction, concerning divine things that were before unknown; an uncovering; an unveiling or revealing.
testimony (GRK: μαρτυρέω / mar-too-reh'-o): To bear witness or testify of true evidence; to give a good report.
blessed (GRK: μακάριος / mak-ar'-ee-os): To be blessed or happy; to be envied; To have God's extended benefits and the advantages He confers; an envied believer in a fortunate position (the recipient of God's provisions and favor which literally extends his Grace to them; His benefits that come with receiving and obeying the Lord's in-birthings of faith.
readeth (GRK: ἀναγινώσκω / an-ag-in-oce'-ko): To know certainly, know again, read; To recognize or discern; The one who enables others to relive and re-appreciate what was conveyed or experienced by the original author.
hear (GRK: ἀκούω / ak-oo'-o): To hear, listen; to comprehend by hearing; pass the test of what is heard or reported; to actually listen; to (figuratively) hear God's voice which prompts Him to birth faith within (Romans 10:17).

Reflections on Revelation

LISTEN AND HEAR THE TRUTH

In this introduction of the book of Revelation, John identifies the source of the prophecy to be Jesus Christ, now risen and ascended to Heaven, seated at the right hand of the power of God; He is God. As John begins to record what he has seen and heard, we see his continued commitment to be obedient to Christ, his old friend and companion. John's language and presentation reveal an entirely new view of Christ, based more in Christ's deity and supernatural power. In this vision of Christ, the Lordship factor is revealed, and it depicts the power of God in this fully human and yet completely Godly person. This Jesus is the God of grace and the God of war at the same time. John relays the importance of seeing Christ in power and glory, as Jesus is going to show us something we need to know and understand. John also relays a promise of blessing to those who do this, who seek to know Jesus and the things to come, and who are obedient to consider this teaching. This Jesus is love and grace while at the same time being ominous and all-powerful. As we can imagine, what John saw was exciting, confusing, and at times disturbing to him, yet he tells us this is truth for our instruction. He is testifying to the authenticity of Christ and this path to truth. John is relaying the message that those who hear and understand these words will be prepared for the coming storms of life, as we now know that the end-times started at the resurrection of Christ. John reinforces that he personally has credibility as he walked with Christ. He stayed the course at the cross, and he has the right to see and hear from Jesus. As the recipients of this message of God's grace, we are also to seek God's divine presence to understand his Word. To be able to comprehend this in even the simplest ways is to actually listen to God. The first and greatest command from John is to keep the things we learn and follow them, for the time is near. This vision was the start of modern eschatological study, and it is connected to scriptures that were written thousands of years before. This message is a miracle of God right in front of us; it's visible and powerful. Come join us in discovering God's heart for the past, the present, and the future of the church and the Kingdom of God. Let's find Christ in Revelation, together.

---

1. Is there any significance to how John started this prophecy?
2. What is the message from verse three?
3. If these things must shortly take place, how can this message be relevant two thousand years later?
4. How can studying this book give us God's extended benefits and the advantages He confers?
5. What insights did you gain from the word studies from this session?
6. Share your thoughts and questions from this week's study. Discuss the word studies and how to read them.

Assigned for next session: (1) Read Revelation 1 daily; (2) Journal and record your thoughts and questions; (3) Complete session 2 for the next class.

Notes

NOTES

Session 2

FINDING CHRIST IN REVELATION

Revelation 1:4-6 (KJV)

JOHN GREETS THE SEVEN CHURCHES

(4) John to the seven **churches** which are in Asia: Grace be unto you, and peace, from him which is, and which was, and which is to come; and from the seven **Spirits** which are before his throne; **(5)** And from Jesus Christ, who is the **faithful witness**, and the **first begotten** of the dead, and the **prince** of the **kings of the Earth.** Unto him that loved us, and washed us from our sins in his own blood, **(6)** And hath made us kings and **priests** unto God and his Father; to him be glory and dominion **for ever and ever**. Amen.

---

churches (GRK: ἐκκλησία / ek-klay-see'-ah): An assembly or congregation, corporately including the entirety of Christian believers; those called out from the world-unto God; the mystical body of Christ.
spirits (GRK: πνεῦμα / pneu-mah): Wind, spirit, the breath of God that animates life.
faithful (GRK: πιστός / pis-tos'): Reliable, trustworthy, the fullness of the faith God imparts.
witness (GRK: μάρτυς/mar'-toos): One who sees and hears the truth; one who is mindful and heeds God's warnings.
first-begotten (GRK: πρωτότοκος/ pro-tot-ok'-os): The Eldest; The pre-eminent one who first received glorification (resurrection); the unequivocal Sovereign ruler over all creation; first among others (who follow).
prince (Lit: Ruler)(GRK: ἄρχων/ ar'-khone): The Chief Governor; The leader of the assembly of elders; The Chief commander with authority and influence over His jurisdiction.
Kings of the Earth (GRK: βασιλεία/ bas-il-i'-ah): Kingdom, the realm of sovereign-royal power; Authority and rule both in the world, and in the hearts of men.
priest (GRK: ἱερεύς / hei-ayer-yooce): One who offers sacrifice to a God; Sacred one belonging to God's Temple; One who oversees the Sacred Rites of God's Dwelling.
ages (ever and ever) (GRK: αἰών / a-hee-ohn): The Messianic time; a cycle (of time) or series of ages stretching to infinity. (This new age was identified by Christ Baptizing His followers in The Holy Spirit at Pentecost).

Reflections on Revelation

JOHN STARTS WITH GRACE AND PEACE

In these verses John greets the churches in Asia Minor. This is a formal greeting that emphasizes God's peace and grace, and it reaffirms that the church has a special place in God's kingdom. This very special place is still relevant to the church today, and just as John is commanded to send these letters to those churches, he also is preparing the church throughout all of history to receive God's message. This message is being sent to the kings and priests of the church, and John's authority to speak for God is not in doubt. The One Who Is of Every Age, Jesus, is at the right hand of God's power, and He has appointed John to be seated there with Him through the grace and peace that John now writes about. By association, all of the church throughout history also shares this place with God. This Christ is the man who hung broken before John's eyes on the cross and, through that obedience, is now the risen and powerful Savior; he is John's greatest love. The church is the entity that God has entrusted to oversee the sacred rites of the faith, and this message was destined to become part of the Word of God. It is the culmination of what we now know as the Holy Bible, and it is sent to the New Testament Church. By their faithfulness and sacrifice, this message has survived the ages and is now given to us today. This chain of authority has brought salvation to all who have believed, and we can find Jesus in this, the instruction book to the church. It is our guide to fulfill the Great Commission and it is the manual for the Christian life.

---

1. How do we balance our understanding of the authority of the church and our own personal walk with God?
2. If we are kings and priests of God's kingdom, and we command His authority, what impact should this knowledge have on us?
3. What insights did you gain from the word studies in this session?
4. Share your thoughts and questions from this week's study.

Assigned for next session: (1) Read Revelation 1 daily; (2) Journal and record your thoughts and questions; (3) Complete session 3 for the next class.

NOTES

Notes

Session 3

FINDING CHRIST IN REVELATION

Revelation 1:7-8 (KJV)

THE ALPHA AND THE OMEGA

(7) Behold, he cometh with clouds; and every eye shall see him, and they also which pierced him: and all **kindreds** of the Earth **shall wail** because of him. Even so, Amen. **(8)** I am Alpha and Omega, the **beginning** and the ending, saith the Lord, which is, and which was, and which is to come, **the Almighty**.

kindreds (GRK: φυλή / foo-lay): a clan or tribe; race of people; lineage; the descendants of a common ancestor, the progeny springing from Jacob (Israel).

shall wail (GRK: κόπτω / kop'-to): to mourn; to cut (off), strike, to smite; to beat your breast or head in lamentation; lament; mourned; To be incised (struck), resulting in severance or being cut off; to mourn with a cutting sense of personal, tragic loss; To cut to the heart.

beginning (GRK: ἀρχή / ar-khay'): The start or the origin of rule (kingly or magisterial); the initial (starting) point; what comes first and therefore is chief (foremost) and has the priority ahead of the rest; preeminent.

the Almighty (GRK: παντοκράτωρ/ pan-tok-rat-ore): The ruler of all universe; The source of unrestricted power; The One who exercises absolute dominion; The one who holds sway over all things.

Reflections on Revelation

JESUS IS ALIVE AND WELL, ON THE THRONE

In this "introduction" John is relaying to the churches a direct message from Jesus Christ. He is quoting Jesus' very words that He is the All-Powerful One, and with His authority He is announcing that He is not going to sit back and allow sin to corrupt His creation forever. This prophesy from Christ, that He will come again and put an end to the reign of sin, is a reinforcement of the command to fulfill the Great Commission. With this knowledge, and with this insight, their purpose is set; they are to continue to take the Good News, or Gospel, to the world, no matter the cost. Here, as in all of Revelation, we see this central teaching that Jesus is alive and well, he's not dead as the world believes. And as the Son of God He's not an allegory or a symbol. He has within Himself, and He gives to those who believe, a purpose. This purpose is based in His authority to rule, and every human who breathed a breath will know He is Lord. For the churches that John is writing to, this message is a confirmation that all the foundations of faith they are risking their lives for will be worth more than anything this world can take from them (2 Corinthians 6:18). Jesus is coming again, and it won't be in secret, and even those who rejected Him, scourged Him, and crucified Him will see Him in all His power and glory (Mark 14:62; Acts 7:54-59). The very clouds that lead the Children of Israel through the wilderness, that encompassed Christ at His transfiguration, and which ushered Jesus up to Heaven in the ascension, will also surround His second coming. This second arrival will be a very real awakening for the world. Christ is surrounded with God's power and He will no longer allow Himself to be vulnerable to death or evil; He has conquered both. The earthly kingdoms will suffer a great loss and will smite themselves for their stupidity and for their rejection of Jesus as Messiah. He is forever, the only true reality, and those who rejected Him throughout time will lament their blindness and lack of faith. They will be cut off from peace and will suffer a tragic loss, including eternal death, yet they will retain the ability to think, reason, and feel loss. We can see here that to find Christ now, in this day and age, is very important. He is the one who gives life purpose in a mundane and evil world.

1. What will it be like to see Jesus coming to change everything?
2. To the church of that day, and today, what might this message mean?
3. How can a church survive without unity?
4. What does verse seven say to you?
5. These verses reference the past, the present, and the future of the church; What should this mean to the church today?
6. What insights did you gain from the word studies in this session?
7. Share your thoughts and questions from this week's study.

Assigned for next session: (1) Read Revelation chapter one daily; (2) Journal and record thoughts and questions; (3) Complete session four for the next class.

Notes

NOTES

Session 4

FINDING CHRIST IN THE BOOK OF REVELATION

Revelation 1:9-20 (KJV)

JOHN'S SPIRITUAL VISION OF CHRIST

(9) I John, who also am your brother, and **companion** in **tribulation**, and in the kingdom and patience of Jesus Christ, was in the isle that is called Patmos, for the word of God, and for the testimony of Jesus Christ. **(10)** I was in the Spirit on the Lord's day, and heard behind me a great voice, as of a trumpet, **(11)** Saying, I am Alpha and Omega, the first and the last: and, What thou seest, write in a book, and send it unto the seven churches which are in Asia; unto Ephesus, and unto Smyrna, and unto Pergamos, and unto Thyatira, and unto Sardis, and unto Philadelphia, and unto Laodicea. **(12)** And I turned to see the voice that spake with me. And being turned, I saw seven golden candlesticks; **(13)** And in the midst of the seven candlesticks one like unto the **Son of man**, clothed with a garment down to the foot, and girt about the paps with a golden girdle. **(14)** His head and his hairs were white like wool, as white as snow; and his eyes were as a **flame of fire**; **(15)** And his feet like unto fine brass, as if they burned in a furnace; and his voice as the sound of many waters. **(16)** And he had in his right hand seven stars: and out of his mouth went a sharp two-edged sword: and his countenance was as the sun shineth in his strength. **(17)** And when I saw him, I fell at his feet as dead. And he laid his right hand upon me, saying unto me, Fear not; I am the first and the last: **(18)** I am he that liveth, and was dead; and, behold, I am alive for evermore, Amen; and have the keys of Hell and of death. **(19)** Write the things which thou hast seen, and the things which are, and the things which shall be hereafter; **(20)** The mystery of the seven stars which thou sawest in my right hand, and the seven golden candlesticks. The seven stars are the angels of the seven churches: and the seven candlesticks which thou sawest are the seven churches.

---

companion (GRK: συνκοινωνὸς/ soong-koy-no-nos): A fellow partaker; one who is partaking jointly; a co-partner and close companion.

tribulation (GRK: θλῖψις /thlip-sis): Persecution, affliction, distress; pressure that constricts or rubs together; a narrow place that "hems someone in"; without options or escape.

Son of man (GRK: υἱὸν ἀνθρώπου / hwee-on anthro-poo): The Son, Descendant of all; Eternal One; the redemption of all, inclusive of all (John 15:5; Eze 1:26; Dan 7:13; Mat. 24:30; Mat. 26:64; Mark 13:26).

flame of fire (GRK: φλὸξ πυρός / phlox poor-os): Flame like the heat of the sun; strife or trials that purify; the eternal transforming fire of God that turns all into light; Enlightenment that purifies; uninterrupted privilege of experiencing faith.

Reflections on Revelation

LISTEN AND HEAR THE TRUTH

What seems to be the central theme here is that Christ is among the churches, which are represented by the lampstands, and He is again seen as ominous and powerful. He is the all-powerful God and Lord over all things. That's not to say that He's not still connected to His human existence. He's fully God and fully man, and He's still a risen Savior. Because of His obedience even unto death, He has the right to save all who will choose Him, to regenerate their spiritual (and someday, their physical) lives. He has defeated death for all time and all who believe in Him are redeemed and descended from Him; they will always be (John 14:20). The churches here represent all who were and all who will be part of God's holy people. There is a current and future plan that will be completed. It started at the tree of the knowledge of good and evil and at the fall of man, when sin entered this world, and it will continue to move towards completion. The message is the miracle of salvation, the redemption of the Cross, and the born-again life. Jesus has the keys to unlock Hell, to eliminate death for all who will receive this gift. The seven churches have seven guardian angels watching over them, and Jesus is using John to assure the church, to say to all, that "I am with you and you will never die." We can find this commitment from Jesus today as he is still saying to the church, "I am here."

---

1. Is the modern church covered by guardian angels?
2. Why does the church suffer tribulation if it is part of the all-powerful Kingdom of God?
3. Why does John fall at the feet of Christ in fear as if he were playing dead?
4. What insights did you gain from the word studies in this session?
5. Share your thoughts and questions from this week's study.

Assigned for next session: (1) Read Revelation chapter two daily; (2) Journal and record thoughts and questions; (3) Complete session five for next class.

NOTES

Notes

SESSION 5

FINDING CHRIST IN THE BOOK OF REVELATION

REVELATION 2:1-7 (KJV)

FIRST LOVE IS SERVING CHRIST

(1) Unto the angel of the church of Ephesus write; These things saith he that holdeth the seven stars in his right hand, who walketh in the midst of the seven golden candlesticks; **(2) I know** thy **works**, and thy labour, and thy patience, and how thou canst not **bear** them which are evil: and thou hast **tried** them which say they are apostles, and are not, and hast found them liars: **(3)** And hast borne, and hast patience, and for my name's sake hast laboured, and hast not fainted. **(4)** Nevertheless I have somewhat against thee, because thou **hast left** thy **first love**. **(5)** Remember therefore from whence thou art **fallen**, and **repent**, and do the first works; or else I will come unto thee quickly, and will remove thy candlestick out of his place, except thou repent. **(6)** But this thou hast, that thou hatest the deeds of the Nicolaitanes, which I also hate. **(7)** He that hath an ear, let him hear what the Spirit saith unto the churches; To him that **overcometh** will I give to eat of the tree of life, which is in the midst of the paradise of God.

I know (GRK: οἶδα / i'-do): To be aware of; to perceive; (in the perfect tense, already completed); to remember; prevent fading; to appreciate; to see physically a metaphorical truth; to perceive or grasp spiritual truth.
works (GRK: ἔργον / er'-gon): A task or vocation; active employment that requires action; wrought or made; to accomplish from an inner desire, intention and purpose.
bear (GRK: βαστάζω/bas-tad'-zo): Not able to take up or carry; unable to endure or tolerate.
Tried (GRK: πειράζω/pi-rad'-zo): A trial; tested; proven through examination.
hast left (GRK: ἀφῆκες / af-ee'-Kes): Abandoned; to consciously send away; discharge; let go of; release; permit to depart; to remit; to forgive; to permit suffering.
first (GRK: πρώτην / pro-tain): The first, principal, and most important; foremost.
love (GRK: ἀγάπην / agap-ain): Benevolence and good will; the esteem which centers in God's moral preferences.
Fallen (GRK: πίπτω / pip'-to): To fall, as under condemnation; to fall prostrate; to beat down.
repent (GRK: μετανοέω / met-an-o-eh'-o): To change one's mind and purpose; To change the inner man (particularly with reference to acceptance of the will of God); To think differently afterwards.
overcomes (GRK: νικῶντι / nik-awn-tee): to conquer, to prevail; to be victorious; to overcome and subdue; earn victory in a great battle.

REFLECTIONS ON REVELATION

LOVE THE LORD AND FULFILL THE GREAT COMMISSION

The church in Ephesus had done a great work in continuing the ministry Paul started there on his second missionary journey. They established a community of believers that had grown and survived for some 30 to 40 years. God's anointing was obviously on this ministry but then something changed. We do not know what specifically, but we can infer, using the definitions from the word studies, that Jesus' message was to find their first love again. Since Jesus mentions works, we can assume this meant, at least in part, that the work of ministry to advance the Kingdom had lost intentionality and purpose. Many believe complacency had set in, and this was a reminder to this church, and to all church bodies, to always maintain their eternal focus. The church is to never let the vision and purpose of the Great Commission die; the church should always be outward looking (Matthew 28:16-20). John reminds this congregation that they are in the hands of Christ, He holds the power that keeps them, and He is walking with them. To walk means to go somewhere, to set your purpose in reaching that destination. The message to the church is that if the love of Jesus we have received from the Spirit of God drives us forward, the evangelical message will always be in the forefront of our purpose. This one message combining love, grace, redemption, justification and salvation that we call the Gospel must not be lost. Our first love is for Jesus, and for those who do not know Him we desire for them to find their names written in the Lamb's Book of Life. As we find Christ in our daily lives, let's share that joy with others.

---

1. How does God's holy church consciously abandon the Great Commission?
2. What constitutes an apostle and does the church still have apostles today?
3. How does personal discipleship affect the church as a whole?
4. What insights did you gain from the word studies in this session?
5. Share your thoughts and questions from this week's study.

Assigned for next session: (1) Read Revelation chapter two daily; (2) Journal and record thoughts and questions; (3) Complete session six for next class.

Notes

NOTES

Session 6

FINDING CHRIST IN THE BOOK OF REVELATION

Revelation 2:8-11 (KJV)

EXPECT PERSECUTION

(8) And unto the angel of the church in Smyrna write; These things saith the first and the last, which was dead, and is alive; **(9)** I know thy works, and tribulation, and **poverty**, (but thou art **rich**) and I know the **blasphemy** of them which say they are Jews, and are not, but are the synagogue of Satan. **(10)** Fear none of those things which thou shalt suffer: behold, the devil shall cast some of you into prison, that ye may be **tried**; and ye shall have tribulation ten days: be thou faithful unto death, and I will give thee a crown of life. **(11)** He that hath an ear, let him hear what the Spirit saith unto the churches; He that overcometh shall not be hurt of the **second death**.

---

poverty (GRK: πτωχεία / pto-khi'-ah): Beggary, destitute of riches; extreme poverty.
rich (GRK: πλούσιος / ploo'-see-os): Abounding in wealth; fully resourced; having God's abundance that comes from receiving His provisions (material and spiritual riches) through faith.
blasphemy (GRK: βλασφημία/ blas-fay-me'-ah): To slander; to use abusive or scurrilous language; sluggish and slow to call something good that really is good, and slow to identify what is truly bad (that really is evil). Someone who switches right for wrong and wrong for right; calls what God disapproves of as right and exchanges the truth of God for a lie (Romans chapter 1:1-32).
tried (GRK: πειράζω/ pi-rad'-zo): To test or prove, to attempt to test; to try before a court. (Mt 4:11; Lk 22:28; 1 Cor 10:13; Js 1:12).
second death (GRK: θανάτου / than'-at-os): The death that can be both physical or spiritual; separation from the life (salvation) of God forever by dying without first dying to self to receive His gift of salvation.

Reflections on Revelation

THE CHURCH WILL SUFFER FOR THE FAITH

In these verses Jesus is openly honest about how important human perspective can be, especially for the persecuted saints of the church. Today, many Christians never truly experience persecution, not the kind that demands your life. Jesus' message does not include any worldly deliverance or reward, but we can still find value in his message. It is based in eternal kingdom riches, and in the knowledge that the God of the universe is on your side, meaning that a better destiny awaits you. Jesus emphasizes that trials and tribulations in this world are normal, and He is specific that faith sometimes even requires death. Satan, the enemy of the church, directs all of the spiritual and physical attacks against the Kingdom of God. All blood-bought Christians will be in the path of that attack because Satan wants to destroy the Church. It's his best leverage towards harming God. Jesus commands this church, and by association all churches, to give up all they have here on Earth for The Crown of Life in the Kingdom of God. Only true faith and dedication to belief in the Kingdom of God could make this an acceptable sacrifice! Most who do this study are raised in western freedoms, where there is wealth and a love for life. Family and position are taken for granted by many in the free world and we believe it is the right of the children of God to have all of these blessings. However, Jesus paints a different perspective in these verses of a church that is placing it all on the line for their faith. This perspective is not always a popular one, but it is a necessary one, and this message is relevant today, to all of God's Church, to continue to do whatever it takes to spread the Gospel to the entire world and to support our fellow saints who are giving their lives for the Gospel while we enjoy our lives. While the missionary journeys continue, find a way to get involved in that mission and join the work to take Christ to a lost world.

---

1. What does Jesus suggest the Christians in Smyrna do when persecution comes?
2. If we are blessed with wealth and comfort, should we carry a sense of guilt over Christians who do not have these advantages? What, if anything, can we do for them?
3. What insights did you gain from the word studies in this session?
4. Share your thoughts and questions from this week's study.

Assigned for next session: (1) Read Revelation chapter two daily; (2) Journal and record thoughts and questions; (3) Complete session seven for next class.

NOTES

NOTES

Session 7

FINDING CHRIST IN THE BOOK OF REVELATION

Revelation 2:12-17 (NKJV)

EVIL PURSUITS IN THE CHURCH

(12) And to the angel of the church in Pergamos write; These things saith he which hath the sharp sword with **two edges; (13)** I know thy works, and where thou **dwellest,** even where Satan's seat is: and thou holdest fast my name, and hast not denied my faith, even in those days wherein Antipas was my faithful martyr, who was slain among you, where Satan dwelleth. **(14)** But I have a few things against thee, because thou hast there them that hold the **doctrine** of Balaam, who taught Balac to cast a stumbling block before the children of Israel, to eat things sacrificed unto idols, and **to commit fornication. (15)** So hast thou also them that hold the doctrine of the Nicolaitanes, which thing I hate. **(16) Repent;** or else I will come unto thee quickly, and will fight against them with the sword of my mouth. **(17)** He that hath an ear, let him hear what the Spirit saith unto the churches; To him that overcometh will I give to eat of the hidden manna, and will give him a white stone, and in the stone a new name written, which no man knoweth saving he that receiveth it.

---

two-edged (GRK: δίστομος / dis'-tom-os): Double-mouthed; A sharp sword; a drinker of blood; to penetrates at every point of contact, a sword that is ideal for defensive or offensive use.

dwellest (GRK: κατοικέω / kat-oy-keh'-o): To inhabit; to permanently reside; fixed dwelling; personal residence; exactly at home; existing; perfectly aligned.

doctrine (GRK: διδαχή/did-akh-ay'): An established teaching; summarized body of respected teaching; reliable and time-honored; a systematic theology.

to commit fornication (GRK: πορνεύω / porn-yoo'-o): To commit sexual immorality; practice idolatry of the flesh; to be unfaithful; a poser of commitment to Christ; to justify a lifestyle of sin.

repent (GRK: μετανοέω / met-an-o-eh'-o): To change your mind and purpose; change the inner man; accepting the will of God; think differently afterwards.

Reflections on Revelation

THE HIDDEN MANNA, WHITE STONE, NEW NAME

In this message to the church in Pergamos, Jesus addresses the idolatry of false doctrines, which is rebellion and evil behavior. He is exposing the sin that had infiltrated the thoughts, deeds, and teaching of the congregation and had contradicted the exclusionary doctrine of Christ, of not allowing other religions to influence Christianity. The message seems to have a very stern warning against falling away from the given Word, a theme that is carried throughout Revelation. It's obvious that the doctrines of false religions had seeped into the church, maybe with little resistance or maybe with a lot, but the warning is to have none! The doctrine of sin was obviously important for the church to follow but was not respected by the culture of the time; it was seen as an attack on the accepted right to sin in the name of religion. This warning was to stop that sin from infiltrating the doctrines of Christianity, to protect the church's entire being! Jesus commands us to change our minds and our thinking about this, so this could only mean these doctrines had been accepted at a level that had affected the church's thoughts and behaviors; it was compromise into sin and had been accepted by many! The solution offered was to change their minds about this, to think differently. For centuries the Church has taught that to repent means to turn around, 180 degrees, but the literal meaning is to "change your mind," and this is Christ's call to all. The white stone represents acquittal in a court of law and the hidden manna is God's secret grace and forgiveness when you go to Him in private and confess with the intention of surrender to repentance. The new name seems to be akin to the name written in the Lamb's Book of Life, it is assigned when you received Christ and because of the struggles you have endured. This new name is a warring name which calls you to the fight to share Christ. Jesus is calling them, and us, to battle, and we know who wins!

---

1. Is Jesus' reference to a two-edged sword (Rev. 2:12) a threat? Why would Jesus issue such a threatening statement?
2. What compromises have we seen in the church in our evil days? (2 Tim 3:1-9)
3. What is the true nature of repentance, and how should it affect our lives?
4. What insights did you gain from the word studies in this session?
5. Share your thoughts and questions from this week's study.

Assigned for next session: (1) Read Revelation chapter two daily; (2) Journal and record thoughts and questions; (3) Complete session eight for next class.

NOTES

Notes

Session 8

FINDING CHRIST IN THE BOOK OF REVELATION

Revelation 2:18-29 (KJV)

CONFRONTING SIN IN THE CHURCH

(18) And unto the angel of the church in Thyatira write; These things saith the Son of God, who hath his eyes like unto a flame of fire, and his feet are like fine brass; **(19)** I know thy works, and charity, and **service**, and faith, and thy **patience**, and thy works; and the last to be more than the first. **(20)** Notwithstanding I have a few things against thee, because thou sufferest that woman **Jezebel**, which calleth herself a prophetess, to teach and to seduce my servants to commit fornication, and to eat things sacrificed unto idols. **(21)** And I gave her space to repent of her fornication; and she repented not. **(22)** Behold, I will cast her into a bed, and them that commit adultery with her into Great Tribulation, except they repent of their deeds. **(23)** And I will kill her children with death; and all the churches shall know that I am he which searcheth the reins and hearts: and I will give unto every one of you according to your works. **(24)** But unto you I say, and unto the rest in Thyatira, as many as have not this doctrine, and which have not known the depths of Satan, as they speak; I will put upon you none other **burden**. **(25)** But that which ye have already **hold fast** till I come. **(26)** And he that overcometh, and keepeth my works unto the end, to him will I give power over the nations: **(27)** And he shall rule them with a rod of iron; as the vessels of a potter shall they be broken to shivers: even as I received of my Father. **(28)** And I will give him the morning star. **(29)** He that hath an ear, let him hear what the Spirit saith unto the churches.

---

service (GRK: διακονίαν / dia-ko-nian): Ministry; waiting at tables; active and done willingly; voluntary attitude; Spirit empowered service guided by faith; the Lord's in-birthed persuasion; close connection of faith.
patience (GRK: ὑπομονήν/hoop-om-on-ayn): To persevere; remain patient, enduring, steadfast; God enabled endurance; endure God's Challenges in life.
Jezebel (GRK:'Ιεζάβελ / ee-ed-zab-ale'): Symbolic name for a false prophetess; One who promotes sexual immorality or idol worship in the church.
burden (GRK: βάρος / bar'-os): Weight; heavy responsibility with personal and eternal significance
hold fast (GRK: κρατήσατε / krat-eh'-sa0te): Be strong; to rule the self; be master of self; to prevail; take hold of; to place under one's grasp or seize hold of to put under control.

Reflections on Revelation

JESUS IS GUARDING THE CHURCH

In these verses Jesus confronts corruption, false doctrines, idol worship, sexual immorality, and all sin-based lifestyles, both in the physical and spiritual existences in the church. These verses are the only in Revelation where Jesus refers to Himself as the Son of God, which signifies that He is the rightful judge of the intentions in the church. He has eyes of flame that see and discern all that happens in the life of the church. Jesus does not seem to be contradicting the redemptive process over sin, which is available for each believer. Instead, he is confronting the false doctrines that have infiltrated the church. When the Spirit-led Christian sins, they know it, and that is when the Holy Spirit reminds them to repent and follow. God's grace is still the source of rescue, but only through repentance and change, then restoration and grace. If repentance is denied, then sin must be exposed and dealt with. The warnings here confront the justification of sin as a means of spreading false religion, leading to ineffectiveness and powerlessness. The term "feet like fine brass" in verse eighteen represents the authority with which Jesus leads and judges the church, and all things. God will work to invite His children to achieve repentance and grace; however, if you are leading others into rebellion in the church and you refuse to repent, God will deal with you. God loves all but must defend the Church from corruption and sin. Those who repent and follow will rule with Christ. Their sin is converted to grace because of repentance and surrender. Never underestimate the importance of obedience! Listen and learn from the Holy Spirit, then obey. Find Christ in this struggle to be like Him, and make sure you submit to the authority and accountability from the Church over you.

---

1. How do we guard against false doctrines of sin infiltrating the church?
2. Who was Jezebel and what was this sin? (I and 2 Kings; Rev 8:20)
3. What kind of death is found in verse 23?
4. What insights did you gain from the word studies in this session?
5. Share your thoughts and questions from this week's study.

Assigned for next session: (1) Read Revelation chapter three daily; (2) Journal and record thoughts and questions; (3) Complete session nine for next class.

NOTES

NOTES

Session 9

FINDING CHRIST IN THE BOOK OF REVELATION

Revelation 3:1-6 (KJV)

THE COMMAND TO OVERCOME

(1) And unto the angel of the church in Sardis write; These things saith he that hath the seven Spirits of God, and the seven stars; I know thy works, that thou hast a **name** that thou livest, and art dead. **(2)** Be **watchful**, and **strengthen** the things which remain, that are ready to die: for I have not found thy works **perfect** before God. **(3)** Remember therefore how thou hast received and heard, and hold fast, and repent. If therefore thou shalt not watch, I will come on thee as a thief, and thou shalt not know what hour I will come upon thee. **(4)** Thou hast a few names even in Sardis which have not defiled their garments; and they shall walk with me in white: for they are worthy. **(5)** He that overcometh, the same shall be clothed in white raiment; and I will not blot out his name out of the book of life, but I will confess his name before my Father, and before his angels. **(6)** He that hath an ear, let him hear what the Spirit saith unto the churches.

---

name (GRK: ὄνομα / on'-om-ah): Literal: "The Characterization;" a name of authority and cause; a name with character, fame, and reputation; figuratively-the manifestation or revelation of someone's character that distinguishing them from all others.
watchful (GRK: γρηγορῶν /gray-gor-yone) To be awake (holds to being sober and serious); watchful as on the alert; to be vigilant and responsible.
strengthen (GRK: στήρισον / stay-ri-son) To make fast or establish; to fix firmly in the right direction; To be self-directed; To generally prop up and support; to set fast or fix (as in concrete); to secure and firmly establish (which eliminates the inability to decide correctly between different opinions or actions; to resolve indecision!
perfect (GRK: πεπληρωμένα / pep-leir-ōmen-a) To make full, to complete, fill to individual capacity; To fully accomplish; supply liberally.

Reflections on Revelation

THE CASUAL, HYPOCRITICAL CHURCH

In these verses Jesus is confronting casual Christianity and the death of mission purpose in the church. In the culture that this was written, a person's name was their title. It revealed a person's character and reputation (Prov. 22:1). Jesus now applies this understanding to the spiritual lives of the church and teaches that if you carry God's Name with you then your character and integrity need to be found in God's purpose for your life. The message is that you can be physically alive while at the same time being spiritually dead. Remember the Pharisees and Sadducees were like this, and Jesus set about to expose their hypocrisy. Jesus is critiquing the intention of those in the church who are not evangelical in their understanding of God's mission for them. The church is to be outward looking in order to fulfill the Great Commission. This teaching is a call to overcome casual Christianity. It is a reminder that the church, as God's children, is to seek approval through their commitment to missions, not through selfish pursuits. If we are sober and intentional about walking in the instruction of Christ, then we will be able to complete the work God gives us to do. If not, the church's purpose has died. And if this is the case, then Jesus tells the church that he will come to them as a thief, and in God's Word this usually means in judgement. Jesus wants to be with his followers in spiritual intimacy and in purpose. He is the Bridegroom and the Church is the bride (Matt. 25:1-13). If a church loses its appropriate motivation and stops completing the Great Commission, then it is dead in its relationship with Christ. Jesus then will come as a thief and not as the Bridegroom. There is hope, though. We can always turn back to the work God has given. The church can find Christ in these verses by seeing His desire to keep his children from the destruction of complacency. This is a message that Jesus saves and gives purpose for life.

---

1. What is Jesus' problem with the church in Sardis, and how does this apply to the church today?
2. Discuss what name and reputation the Church caries today, and are the negative views of the church completely the fault of the church?
3. What can a person, or church do, to take on the mission of Christ?
4. What insights did you gain from the word studies in this session?
5. Share your thoughts and questions from this week's study.

Assigned for next session: (1) Read Revelation chapter three daily; (2) Journal and record thoughts and questions; (3) Complete session 10 for next class.

Notes

NOTES

Session 10

FINDING CHRIST IN THE BOOK OF REVELATION

Revelation 3:7-13 (KJV)

THE OBEDIENT CHURCH

(7) And to the angel of the church in Philadelphia write; These things saith he that is **holy**, he that is **true**, he that hath the **key** of David, he that openeth, and no man shutteth; and shutteth, and no man openeth; **(8)** I know thy works: behold, I have set before thee an open door, and no man can shut it: for thou hast a little **strength**, and hast kept my word, and hast not denied my name. **(9)** Behold, I will make them of the synagogue of Satan, which say they are Jews, and are not, but do lie; behold, I will make them to come and worship before thy feet, and to know that I have loved thee. **(10)** Because thou hast kept the word of my **patience**, I also will keep thee from the hour of temptation, which shall come upon all the world, to try them that dwell upon the Earth. **(11)** Behold, I come quickly: hold that fast which thou hast, that no man take thy crown. **(12)** Him that overcometh will I make a pillar in the temple of my God, and he shall go no more out: and I will write upon him the name of my God, and the name of the city of my God, which is new Jerusalem, which cometh down out of Heaven from my God: and I will write upon him my new name. **(13)** He that hath an ear, let him hear what the Spirit saith unto the churches.

---

holy (GRK: ἅγιος / hag'-ee-os): Sacred and set apart for God; different and unlike any other; the likeness and nature of God.
true [One] (GRK: ἀληθινός / al-ay-thee-nos'): The One made of Truth; authentic unity with visible fact; the integrity of truth; true inside and out; reality.
key (GRK: κλεῖν / kle-en): The keeper; power to open and to shut the word of God; Power to open or shut the pit of Hell; power of death and life; ultimate authority.
strength (GRK: δύναμις / doo'-nam-is): Miraculous might; physical force and ability; efficacy; energy for marvelous works.
patience (GRK: ὑπομονῆς / hy-po-mon-ais): To persevere; endurance; steadfastness; patient waiting; able to remain.

Reflections on Revelation

THE CHURCH THAT KEEPS THE FAITH

In these verses Jesus again reaffirms His position of power in God's Kingdom. His qualification to fulfill prophesy as the Messiah is verified in His lineage from Abraham as a child of Israel, and King David, whom his mother was descended from. In the Eternal Kingdom He is the Eternal One who has always been able to direct all things and fulfill all prophesy. The open door in verse eight can be contrasted with Jesus knocking at the closed door of the Laodiceans church later in chapter three; this is evidence that a church can be separated from God according to the condition of the heart, but that Jesus will continue to seek relationship with his bride (2 Cor. 11; Matthew 25:1-13). The door to this church is open and will remain open to God's sustaining power because they have remained faithful with little, and humility opens every door to God for those who walk in the Spirit (Gal. 5). Their reward is to be saved from the hour of temptation (Vs 10), which is possibly a reference to the rapture and taking up of the church, or it may refer to God's blessed covering that will shield them from the judgements of the tribulation. The keys, and the open door, reaffirm God's ownership of the church and of His children. They overcome temptation by the desire of their hearts placed there by the Holy Spirit. Now verse nine is very interesting; Jesus jumps from the recognition of the church in Philadelphia to the condemnation of the Judaic religion and political power of Jerusalem. This leadership has continued to persecute the church and has even joined Rome in this persecution. The once chosen people, in association with their political and religious leaders' rejection of their Messiah, has turned the temple, once the dwelling place of God, into the dwelling place of evil. Even today, all who participate in rejecting Jesus as Lord, and who deny the work of the Holy Spirit (Mark 3:28-30), will learn humility by judgement. Remember, the obedient church is made of those who overcome, they remain in God's strength though they are weak, they persevere in trials, and they keep the faith. This is how Christ is found today, by walking in the path of humility, obedience, and faithfulness.

---

1. What does it mean to be kept from the hour of temptation?
2. What is God's plan for Israel at this point in Revelation?
3. What insights did you gain from the word studies in this session?
4. Share your thoughts and questions from this week's study.

Assigned for next session: (1) Read Revelation chapter three daily; (2) Journal and record thoughts and questions; (3) Complete session 11 for next class.

NOTES

Notes

Session 11

FINDING CHRIST IN THE BOOK OF REVELATION

Revelation 3:14-22 (KJV)

THE LUKEWARM CHURCH

(14) And unto the angel of the church of the Laodiceans write; These things saith the **Amen**, the faithful and true **witness**, the beginning of the creation of God; **(15)** I know thy works, that thou art neither cold nor hot: I would thou wert cold or hot. **(16)** So then because thou art **lukewarm**, and neither cold nor hot, I will **spue** thee out of my mouth. **(17)** Because thou sayest, I am rich, and increased with goods, and have need of nothing; and knowest not that thou art **wretched**, and **miserable**, and poor, and blind, and naked: **(18)** I **counsel** thee to buy of me gold tried in the fire, that thou mayest be rich; and white raiment, that thou mayest be clothed, and that the shame of thy nakedness do not appear; and anoint thine eyes with eye salve, that thou mayest see. **(19)** As many as I love, I rebuke and chasten: be **zealous** therefore, and repent. **(20)** Behold, I stand at the door, and knock: if any man hear my voice, and open the door, I will come in to him, and will sup with him, and he with me. **(21)** To him that overcometh will I grant to sit with me in my throne, even as I also overcame, and am set down with my Father in his throne. **(22)** He that hath an ear, let him hear what the Spirit saith unto the churches.

---

amen (GRK: ἀμήν / am-ane): True, sure, certain one; agree to let it be so.
witness (GRK: μάρτυς / mar-tys): To see and hear the truth; an eye witness who can testify of the truth.
lukewarm (GRK: χλιαρός/ khlee-ar-os): Tepid and only slightly warm; to be wretched of soul, unenthusiastic, and lethargic.
spue (GRK: ἐμέσαι/ em-es, hai): Spit out or vomit; be repulsed; utter rejection or total separation; divorce.
wretched (GRK: ταλαίπωρος/ tal-ahee-po-ros): Distressed and miserable; afflicted; beaten-down; full of calluses; deep misery from significant hardships.
miserable (GRK: ἐλεεινός/ el-eh-i-nos'): Pitiable and in great need of mercy; desperate.
counsel (GRK: συμβουλεύω/ sym-boul-eh-uo): To take advice; to exhort; consult and plan with resolve; keep pre-set goals; a holy agreement revealed by Christ.
zealous (GRK: ζηλόω/ dzay-lou-oh): To imitate; to ambitiously strive after: to burn with zeal; to boil; to be zealous in the pursuit of good.

Reflections on Revelation

TRUE MINISTRY RESULTS FROM A COMMITTED WALK

The lukewarm faith has been a topic of discussion throughout church history, mostly because of these verses. Here, Jesus leads us into an understanding of what it means to be the outward-looking, evangelical church, and the message is that disciples of Christ, both on a personal basis and on a corporate level, need to avoid complacency. The lukewarm life destroys God's plan for both the individual and the church, as the Great Commission is no longer their goal. Imagine, Christ stands outside the door of His own church, begging to be let in! How can this be? The phrase "I stand" in verse twenty is in the perfect tense, meaning that Jesus stood there in the past, is now standing there, and will always be there, trying to gain access. The word "knock" from verse twenty is in the present tense, which means it is happening at this very moment. Jesus is saying to all that He will not leave or give up until he has unity in heart and purpose with His church. The church is being disciplined and chastened for losing sight of God's mission, for laziness and disobedience, and possibly for shrinking back from persecution. But this is not a separation, it is an invitation to restoration. With open arms God is seeking reconnection in spiritual purpose with His creation. This message displays a deeper love than human understanding can fathom, and it shows God's desire to restore relationship to the church and the individual. For those who have stopped attending church, reading the Bible, or spending time in prayer and worship, this message is paramount for a restored life of faith. Jesus is knocking. Will you answer the door and be an overcomer today?

---

1. What makes a person or a church lukewarm?
2. What traps a church in complacency?
3. If you are lukewarm, what should you do?
4. What does verse twenty-one mean?
5. What insights did you gain from the word studies in this session?
6. Share your thoughts and questions from this week's study.

Assigned for next session: (1) Read Revelation chapter four daily; (2) Journal and record thoughts and questions; (3) Complete session 12 for next class.

NOTES

Notes

Session 12

FINDING CHRIST IN THE BOOK OF REVELATION

Revelation 4:1-11 (KJV)

JOHN SEES THE THRONE ROOM

(1) After this I looked, and, behold, a door was opened in Heaven: and the first voice which I heard was as it were of a trumpet talking with me; which said, Come up hither, and I will shew thee things which must be hereafter. **(2)** And immediately I was in the spirit: and, behold, a throne was set in Heaven, and one sat on the throne. **(3)** And he that sat was to look upon like a jasper and a **sardine** stone: and there was a rainbow round about the throne, in sight like unto an emerald. **(4)** And round about the throne were four and twenty seats: and upon the seats I saw four and twenty elders sitting, clothed in white raiment; and they had on their heads crowns of gold. **(5)** And out of the throne proceeded lightnings and thunderings and voices: and there were seven lamps of fire burning before the throne, which are the seven Spirits of God. **(6)** And before the throne there was a sea of glass like unto crystal: and in the midst of the throne, and round about the throne, were four beasts full of eyes before and behind. **(7)** And the first beast was like a lion, and the second beast like a calf, and the third beast had a face as a man, and the fourth beast was like a flying eagle. **(8)** And the four beasts had each of them six wings about him; and they were full of eyes within: and they rest not day and night, saying, Holy, holy, holy, Lord God Almighty, which was, and is, and is to come. **(9)** And when those beasts give glory and honour and thanks to him that sat on the throne, who liveth for ever and ever, **(10)** The four and twenty **elders** fall down before him that sat on the throne, and worship him that liveth for ever and ever, and cast their crowns before the throne, saying, **(11)** Thou art worthy, O Lord, to receive glory and honour and power: for thou hast created all things, and for thy pleasure they are and were created.

---

sardine (GRK: σαρδίῳ/ sar-di-oh): Carnelian, a semi-precious stone; orange or orange-red variety of chalcedony; blood red; the first stone in the High Priest's breastplate; red jasper (signifying the High Priestly position). **elders** (GRK: πρεσβύτερος / pres-boo-ter-os): An elder of the Christian assembly; a mature man having seasoned judgment (experience). (Not angels)

Reflections on Revelation

IN CHRIST WE WILL SEE AMAZING THINGS

John here describes an open door, like the one open to the church in Philadelphia; and he can either see into the throne room of God or is taken to Heaven, but it seems that when he is asked to come up through the door, he is granted entry into Heaven. The description of things around the throne represents God's connection to Jesus Christ, the Holy Spirit, and to the church. Other places in scripture record open doors in Heaven for viewing (Eze.1:1; Mat. 3:16; Acts 7:56; Rev. 19:11). Here again, John emphasizes that he receives this vision while in the spirit (Rev. 4:2), which is how all revelations from God must be received. The seven spirits (Revelation 1:4; Isa. 11:2; Rev. 5:6) point to the aspects of the one Spirit that is poured out on the Anointed Christ and covering the seven churches; they are the angels of the church. This, along with the creatures that have many eyes, indicates an all-seeing and knowing God, and it paints a picture of the power and holiness of God that drives everything around the throne to worship and honor the King of the universe. (Luke 19:35-40). The 24 elders are not named specifically, but the term is written without capital letters, signifying that John is not seeing them as part of the Godhead. However, they do have a connection to God and the throne; they exist and are seated with Christ. How significant and important must they be to have this honor! They worship God, throwing down their own crowns, signifying again honor, respect, allegiance and commitment. They cherish the gifts of grace and salvation more than riches, and they boldly approach God (Heb 4:16) while still showing respect and honor. Can you imagine this scene, which still exists today? It will be an awesome sight to see and will no doubt drive all to cast down their crowns in the presence of the Living God. Finding Christ here is based in the fact that He is the doorway to God's presence. There is no other (John 10).

---

1. Who do you think the 24 elders are?
2. How do you think you will respond to this scene in Heaven?
3. What insights did you gain from the word studies in this session?
4. Share your thoughts and questions from this week's study.

Assigned for next session: (1) Read Revelation chapter five daily; (2) Journal and record thoughts and questions; (3) Complete session 13 for next class.

Notes

NOTES

Session 13

FINDING CHRIST IN THE BOOK OF REVELATION

Revelation 5:1-7 (KJV)

JESUS TAKES THE SCROLL

(1) And I saw in the right hand of him that sat on the throne a book written within and on the backside, sealed with **seven seals.** **(2)** And I saw a **strong** angel **proclaiming** with a loud voice, Who is **worthy** to open the book, and to loose the seals thereof? **(3)** And no man in Heaven, nor in Earth, neither under the Earth, was able to open the book, neither to look thereon. **(4)** And I wept much, because no man was found worthy to open and to read the book, neither to look thereon. **(5)** And one of the elders saith unto me, Weep not: behold, the Lion of the tribe of Judah, the Root of David, hath **prevailed** to open the book, and to loose the seven seals thereof. **(6)** And I beheld, and, lo, in the midst of the throne and of the four beasts, and in the midst of the elders, stood a Lamb as it had been slain, having seven horns and seven eyes, which are the seven Spirits of God sent forth into all the Earth. **(7)** And he came and took the book out of the right hand of him that sat upon the throne.

---

seven (GRK: ἑπτά/ hep-tah'): Seven; God's perfect and finished work; symbolic completeness of God's will.
seals (GRK: σφραγίς/ sfrag-ece): A seal or signet ring; proof etched or engraved into soft wax or clay to seal a document; confirmed, proved, or authenticated.
strong (GRK: ἰσχυρός/ is-khoo-ros): Mighty; powerful, vehement and sure; engaging and combative; God's power that brings His preferred will; force of faith.
proclaiming (GRK: κηρύσσω/ kay-roos'-so): Herald; go before and announce; preach a message with conviction; persuasively; announce the Gospel in authority and binding knowledge.
worthy (GRK: ἄξιος / ax'-ee-os): Weight of worth; deserving; suitable; assigning matching value; God's balance-scale of truth; a balance-scale.
prevailed (GRK: νικάω/ nik-ah'-o): To conquer or be victorious; to overcome, prevail and subdue; to come off victorious in a battle.

Reflections on Revelation

IN CHRIST ALL IS REVEALED

In this vision, John sees Jesus as the slain lamb who is also the resurrected and powerful Savior. He has full power to accomplish God's plan of redemption. We see the scroll of prophecy in God's hand, and it has writing on both sides, akin to the Ten Commandments. It is sealed with seven seals (Rev. 5:1) representing again God's perfect and completed work. It's a picture of the saving grace that Jesus always represented, is representing, and always will represent. God holds this scroll in His right hand, the hand of favor and strength, and this scroll is so sacred to God that none of the patriarchs of Israel, nor even the Apostles of the early church, who had walked with Christ and were martyred for their faith, could come forward and take the scroll. This record of all of God's finishing plan is so important that when no one can open it John is driven to tears. Then Jesus enters the scene with seven horns of authority and power over the seven churches, and he walks right up to God and takes the scroll. Jesus does not hesitate to assume his place as the Lion of Judah, and this is a major transition point in Revelation that we need to see clearly. The discussion of the restoration of Israel to their Messiah has been introduced, and in this vision, it shows us the new purpose of the end times and the tribulation. It is for the restoration of the chosen people of Israel, which we can assume has something to do with this scroll. Jesus is going to war; however, the goal of his perfect love is not to destroy, but to restore grace to Israel. Only the One Who purchased redemption and Who is without sin can have this kind of love. Judaism will forever be replaced with the Christian faith in the hearts of God's chosen people. Christ is found here in His commitment to keep His Word, and to love in the midst of life-shaking change.

---

1. What did Jesus accomplish to be worthy to open the seven seals from the scroll?
2. Why did John weep when he saw no one opening the scroll?
3. Do you see these verses as a transition into a new theme for the tribulation, and if so, is this when the rapture will happen?
4. How would you respond if Christianity was forever changed to a new covenant? (How did those of the Judaic faith feel?)
5. What insights did you gain from the word studies from this session?
6. Share your thoughts and questions from this week's study.

Assigned: (1) Read Revelation chapter five daily; (2) Journal and record thoughts and questions; (3) Complete session 14 for next class.

NOTES

NOTES

Session 14

FINDING CHRIST IN THE BOOK OF REVELATION

Revelations 5:8-14 (KJV)

JESUS IS WORTHY, HE IS THE LAMB

(8) And when he had taken the book, the four beasts and four and twenty elders **fell down** before the Lamb, having every one of them harps, and golden vials full of odours, which are the prayers of saints. **(9)** And they sung a new song, saying, Thou art worthy to take the book, and to open the seals thereof: for thou wast slain, and hast **redeemed** us to God by thy blood out of every kindred, and tongue, and people, and nation; **(10)** And hast made us unto our God kings and priests: and we shall **reign** on the Earth. **(11)** And I beheld, and I heard the voice of many angels round about the throne and the beasts and the elders: and the number of them was ten thousand times ten thousand, and thousands of thousands; **(12)** Saying with a loud voice, Worthy is the Lamb that was slain to receive power, and riches, and wisdom, and strength, and honour, and glory, and blessing. **(13)** And every creature which is in Heaven, and on the Earth, and under the Earth, and such as are in the sea, and all that are in them, heard I saying, Blessing, and honour, and glory, and power, be unto him that sitteth upon the throne, and unto the Lamb for ever and ever. **(14)** And the four beasts said, Amen. And the four and twenty elders fell down and worshipped him that liveth for ever and ever.

---

fell down (GRK: πίπτω/pip-to): To fall as under condemnation; fall prostrate; to prostrate oneself; to fall down in ruin as of a person rendering homage or worship; To lower self from a high place to a low place with no authority.

redeemed (GRK: ἠγόρασας/ ay-go-ras-as): To buy in the marketplace; to purchase where ownership transfers from seller to buyer (now belongs to the Lord as His unique possession); to purchase all the privileges and responsibilities that go with belonging to Him (being in Christ).

reign (GRK: βασιλεύσουσιν/ bas-il-eus-ous-in): To be king or to reign; to rule or reign over; to exercise kingly power; to exercise the highest influence; to control; to have royal power.

Reflections on Revelation

IN CHRIST WE WILL REIGN

Make no mistakes, the throne room is a place where Christ is King, seated on the throne with God, and the Holy Spirit indwells everything there. In the Hebrew culture, the hour of incense was the time when the prayers of the faithful would be offered up to God while burning incense during the evening and morning sacrifice. It was a symbol of rising requests and praises to God. It seems in this vision that incense is still an important part of the worship of God at the throne, a continual reminder that the final sacrifice has been made in Christ. The prayers of the saints throughout history are not forgotten, they are before God even now. This is a symbol of how important prayer is. It can have an impact on a Heavenly and supernatural level. The new song is intended to signify a major shift in the purpose of the tribulation, as many who study eschatology believe that once the rapture takes place, the entirety of the tribulation and end times will be designated solely for the defeat of evil and the restoration of God's chosen people. At the throne, along with prayer, there is worship and singing. Just as in the Old Testament, when the tribe of Judah would lead the Children of Israel into battle with worship and singing, so now, it seems, we are given a picture of God and Christ preparing for the final battle. By increasing prayer and worship, by taking time to honor God and His power and glory, we do war against evil and can find Christ in Revelation. Now we have a new vocation; we are the priests and kings of the Kingdom of God, with Christ, and by the power of the Spirit we are ministers of this new covenant. Jesus started this prophecy in the Lord's Prayer, asking for the Kingdom to come in power (Matt 5-7).

---

1. In your mind, what is God going to do about Israel in the end times?
2. Does God demand our worship? How will we know how to act when we stand before God?
3. What does redemption do for God's children?
4. What insights did you gain from the word studies from this session?
5. Share your thoughts and questions from this week's study.

Assigned for next session: (1) Read Revelation chapter six daily; (2) Journal and record thoughts and questions; (3) Complete session 15 for next class.

NOTES

Notes

Session 15

FINDING CHRIST IN THE BOOK OF REVELATION

Revelation 6:1-8 (KJV)

THE FIRST FOUR SEALS AND THE FOUR RIDERS

(1) And I saw when the Lamb opened one of the seals, and I heard, as it were the noise of thunder, one of the four beasts saying, Come and see. **(2)** And I saw, and behold a white horse: and he that sat on him had a bow; and a crown was given unto him: and he went forth **conquering**, and to conquer. **(3)** And when he had opened the second seal, I heard the second beast say, Come and see. **(4)** And there went out another horse that was red: and power was given to him that sat thereon to take **peace** from the Earth, and that they should kill one another: and there was given unto him a great sword. **(5)** And when he had opened the third seal, I heard the third beast say, Come and see. And I beheld, and lo a black horse; and he that sat on him had a pair of **balances** in his hand. **(6)** And I heard a voice in the midst of the four beasts say, A measure of wheat for a penny, and three measures of barley for a penny; and see thou hurt not the oil and the wine. **(7)** And when he had opened the fourth seal, I heard the voice of the fourth beast say, Come and see. **(8)** And I looked, and behold a pale horse: and his name that sat on him was **Death**, and **Hell** followed with him. And power was given unto them over the fourth part of the Earth, to kill with sword, and with hunger, and with death, and with the beasts of the Earth.

---

conquering (GRK: νικῶν/ Nick-Own): To conquer; to prevail; to victoriously overcome; to subdue in battle.
peace (GRK: εἰρήνη/ i-ray-nay) Being whole or one; to find quietness and rest; to be sound of mind; to join, tie together into God's gift of wholeness.
balances (GRK: ζυγὸν/ dzoo-gon): A balanced scale; yoke of a heavy burden; unites two as one.
death (GRK: θάνατος/ than'-at-os): Die both physically and spiritually; separation from the life and salvation of God; missing personal death to self.
Hell (GRK: Ἅιδης/ hah-dace): Hades; place of departed spirits; unseen underworld; the invisible realm of the dead; dwelling of the physical and spiritual dead.

Reflections on Revelation

THE APPEARING OF ANTICHRIST

Have you ever heard of the four horsemen of the apocalypse? Well, here they are, and they are symbolic of the earthly judgements God will bring to punish this world. Who these riders are, and what they represent, has been a debate in eschatological studies for some time. Some say the rider on a white horse is the Antichrist and that the others are simply his minions, or angels of destruction. This is a relatively modern interpretation from the past two centuries. Previous to this most doctrines taught that they are God's angels of destruction and that the rider in white could be Jesus himself. Whatever the true identities of these riders, they initiate the judgements that seem to be associated with the Great Tribulation. The rider in white does mimic Christ in many ways, which will be a sign of the Antichrist, however, there are some arguments against this premise. He comes to conquer, but Jesus has already conquered; he has weapons and swords, but we know Jesus' weapon is the Two-Edged Sword; he is given a crown, but Jesus already wears the only true Crown. These angels of destruction are given power over all the Earth, and they will inflict suffering on every tongue and nation and will bring all governments to their knees. Even after these evil times start, many on this Earth will continue to walk in blindness and deception and will continue to be victims of their own reprobate minds (Rom. 1:18-32). This propensity to destruction has been alive in man since the original sin and will be brought to an end by God's mighty hand. Jesus is found here in his description as the Lamb of God, the sacrificial payment for sin that will rescue form this fate any person who chooses faith in Him.

---

1. Identify the beasts that announce the four riders.
2. Discuss the four horsemen. What significance do they have, and who are they?
3. What do the four colors of the horses represent? (Zech. 1:8; 6:2–3).
4. What insights did you gain from the word studies from this session?
5. Share your thoughts and questions from this week's study.

Assigned for next session: (1) Read Revelation chapter six daily; (2) Journal and record thoughts and questions; (3) Complete session 16 for next class.

Notes

Notes

Session 16

FINDING CHRIST IN THE BOOK OF REVELATION

Revelation 6:9-17 (KJV)

THE FIFTH AND SIXTHS SEALS

(9) And when he had opened the fifth seal, I saw under the **altar** the souls of them that were slain for the word of God, and for the **testimony** which they held: **(10)** And they cried with a loud voice, saying, How long, O Lord, holy and true, dost thou not judge and **avenge** our blood on them that dwell on the Earth? **(11)** And white robes were given unto every one of them; and it was said unto them, that they should rest yet for a little season, until their fellow servants also and their brethren, that should be killed as they were, should be fulfilled. **(12)** And I beheld when he had opened the sixth seal, and, lo, there was a great Earthquake; and the sun became black as sackcloth of hair, and the moon became as blood; **(13)** And the stars of Heaven fell unto the Earth, even as a fig tree casteth her untimely figs, when she is shaken of a mighty wind. **(14)** And the Heaven departed as a scroll when it is rolled together; and every mountain and island were moved out of their places. **(15)** And the kings of the Earth, and the great men, and the rich men, and the chief captains, and the mighty men, and every bondman, and every free man, hid themselves in the dens and in the rocks of the mountains; **(16)** And said to the mountains and rocks, Fall on us, and hide us from the face of him that sitteth on the throne, and from the **wrath** of the **Lamb**: **(17)** For the great day of his wrath is come; and who shall be able to stand?

Altar (GRK: θυσιαστήριον / thoo-see-as-tay-ree-on): Place of sacrifice; where God and true, sincere worshipers meet; place of consecration; anywhere the believer communes, hears from God, and obeys; place of faith; the Lord's in-birthed persuasion.

testimony (GRK: μαρτυρία/mar-too-ree'-ah): A witness with evidence; a good reputation.

avenge (GRK: ἐκδικέω/ ek-dik-eh'-o): Vindicate; give justice; defend; completed judgment; appropriate outcomes.

wrath (GRK: ὀργῆς / or-gayes): Wrought out of anger; passion for punishment; vengeance; settled anger; rising from ongoing opposition; passionate against sin; settled indignation.

Lamb (GRK: Ἀρνίου/ ar-nee'-ou) Lamb; a little lamb with diminutive force; was lost; a young lamb; person with pure, innocent, virgin-like, and gentle intentions.

Reflections on Revelation

THE JUDGEMENTS LOOSED, AND THE TRIBULATION

In the last session we introduced a term that was before never recorded in the Bible, the word rapture. This term is associated with the term used by Jesus, "taken up", (Matt. 24:40-44). Here, the fifth seal is broken and the martyrs from church history cry to God for justice and revenge. God honors them with white robes signifying their righteousness; however, he delays vengeance for another time. To the believers of that day, this message of God's faithfulness would have been a comfort as they all knew of, and had experienced, the persecution of the church. Many commentaries say that the fifth seal could be the last historical event from Revelation that has already occurred. Events such as the Resurrection, the Jewish revolts against Rome, the Holocaust, the restoration of Israel as a nation, or the history of martyrdom could be interpreted in this way. We can understand here that God's plan for the tribulation will involve justice for those who give their lives for the faith. At the sixth seal we see many natural and supernatural occurrence come upon the Earth. These events are described and are very frightening to ponder. Although we cannot know exactly what they mean, we can understand what these judgements will be like. Could this be the point in time when all the lost people of Earth come to realize that the universe has a creator? This is a valid question, as these verses seem to agree with those in Matthew where Jesus describes the rapture and the presence of the tribulation (Matt. 24:29-31). How better to come to understand the environment of chaos that will prevail on Earth than to imagine what will happen after millions of people simply disappear. The peace of being in God's saving grace is how we find Christ here.

---

1. Could this be the point in time when all people and nations come to realize that God exists?
2. What is it about God's redemption of man that the world hates and resents so strongly?
3. Discuss your thoughts of the tribulation, the rapture, and the meaning of these verses.
4. What insights did you gain from the word studies in this session?
5. Share your thoughts and questions from this week's study.

Assigned for next session: (1) Read Revelation chapter seven daily; (2) Journal and record thoughts and questions; (3) Complete session 17 for next class.

NOTES

NOTES

Session 17

FINDING CHRIST IN THE BOOK OF REVELATION

Revelation 7:1-8 (KJV)

GOD'S CHOSEN PEOPLE

(1) And after these things I saw four angels standing on the four corners of the Earth, holding the four winds of the Earth, that the wind should not blow on the Earth, nor on the sea, nor on any tree. **(2)** And I saw another angel **ascending** from the east, having the **seal** of the living God: and he cried with a loud voice to the four angels, to whom it was **given** to **hurt** the Earth and the sea, **(3)** Saying, Hurt not the Earth, neither the sea, nor the trees, till we have sealed the servants of our God in their foreheads. **(4)** And I heard the number of them which were sealed: and there were sealed an hundred and forty and four thousand of all the tribes of the children of Israel. **(5)** Of the tribe of Juda were sealed twelve thousand. Of the tribe of Reuben were sealed twelve thousand. Of the tribe of Gad were sealed twelve thousand. **(6)** Of the tribe of Aser were sealed twelve thousand. Of the tribe of Nephthalim were sealed twelve thousand. Of the tribe of Manasses were sealed twelve thousand. **(7)** Of the tribe of Simeon were sealed twelve thousand. Of the tribe of Levi were sealed twelve thousand. Of the tribe of Issachar were sealed twelve thousand. **(8)** Of the tribe of Zabulon were sealed twelve thousand. Of the tribe of Joseph were sealed twelve thousand. Of the tribe of Benjamin were sealed twelve thousand.

---

ascending (GRK: ἀναβαίνω/ an-ab-ah-ee-no): To go up, ascend; to rise, spring up, come up.
seal (GRK: σφραγῖδα/ sphra-gi-da): A seal or a signet, like a ring used to make impression; the seal attests of the proof (i.e. engraving); inscription or impression; that by which anything is confirmed, proved, authenticated.
given or granted (GRK: ἐδόθη/ ed-oth-ay): To put in place; to grant, supply, or furnish what is necessary; give over; deliver to.
hurt (GRK: ἀδικῆσαι/ adzi-kay-sai): To do wrong, act wickedly or unjustly; to injure and harm.

Reflections on Revelation

THE MESSIAH AND THE TRIBES OF ISRAEL

The four corners of Earth and the four winds blowing from all directions symbolizes worldwide events. Some suggest that in these verses we see a vision of God's breath of judgement that has been continually held back by the Spirit of God awaiting this command at the initiation of the Great Tribulation. Whatever your interpretation of these verses, we know that John is describing the coming of judgement on Earth. Some see these angels as the four horsemen again, and even if they are not, we see that the entire Earth is at risk. In these verses we can see very clearly the justification of the doctrine that the end times is about the restoration of Israel to their Messiah. They are still the chosen people under the covenant between God to Abraham, and the Twelve Tribes of Israel are represented here as the Sealed of God. As God is exacting judgement on the Earth, He is still giving Israel His provision, just like He sustained them in the wilderness for forty years before they crossed into the promised land (Ex. 22; Deut. 1). Because of their lack of insight, they must now endure the tribulation, and they seem to be the central focus of all God is doing. The angels who have held back judgement from the Earth throughout history since the fall of man are now free to strike. God will not hold back His wrath any longer and the people of Earth will suffer a great loss. They are punished for the act of worshipping themselves, for worshipping nature and the creation instead of worshipping the Creator, for following sin and idolatry, and for rejecting grace. God is preparing to destroy the idols that they have worshipped, and Israel will be joined with the lost in this turmoil. It has been suggested that these twelve tribes are the remnant from the chosen people that will be restored to faith during the tribulation and will serve the Lamb of God at the battle of Armageddon, to be united at last with their Messiah to defeat sin and evil once and for all. It's interesting that the tribe of Dan is missing from listed tribes and that the tribes of Manasseh and Ephraim are not united in the tribe of Joseph their Father (which is an interesting side study). What is clear is that the descendants of Abraham are still key figures in God's plan for the Eternal Kingdom, even during the tribulation. We can find Christ in knowing that the judgement of the saints will be much different than the judgement of the lost.

---

1. What is your belief of what God is doing with the Nation of Israel during the end times?
2. Who are the four angels, what do they symbolize?
3. What insights did you gain from the word studies from this session?
4. Share your thoughts and questions from this week's study.

Assigned for next session: (1) Read Revelation chapter seven daily; (2) Journal and record questions; (3) Complete session 18 for next class.

Notes

NOTES

SESSION 18

FINDING CHRIST IN THE BOOK OF REVELATION

REVELATION 7:9-17 (KJV)

A MULTITUDE FROM THE GREAT TRIBULATION

(9) After this I beheld, and, lo, a great multitude, which no man could number, of all nations, and kindreds, and **people**, and tongues, stood before the throne, and before the Lamb, clothed with white robes, and palms in their hands; **(10)** And cried with a loud voice, saying, **Salvation** to our God which sitteth upon the throne, and unto the Lamb. **(11)** And all the angels stood round about the throne, and about the elders and the four beasts, and fell before the throne on their faces, and worshipped God, **(12)** Saying, Amen: Blessing, and glory, and **wisdom**, and thanksgiving, and honour, and power, and might, be unto our God for ever and ever. Amen. **(13)** And one of the elders answered, saying unto me, What are these which are arrayed in white robes? and whence came they? **(14)** And I said unto him, Sir, thou knowest. And he said to me, These are they which came out of Great Tribulation, and have washed their robes, and made them white in the blood of the Lamb. **(15)** Therefore are they before the throne of God, and serve him day and night in his temple: and he that sitteth on the throne shall **dwell** among them. **(16)** They shall hunger no more, neither thirst anymore; neither shall the sun light on them, nor any heat. **(17)** For the Lamb which is in the midst of the throne shall feed them, and shall lead them unto living fountains of waters: and God shall wipe away all tears from their eyes.

---

peoples (GRK: λαῶν/ La-ohn): God's chosen people, both Jews and Christians; the people of the Lord, Laity.
salvation (GRK: σωτηρία/ so-tay-ree'-ah): Deliverance unto welfare and prosperity; preservation and safety; God's rescue; Deliver from destruction to God's safety.
wisdom (GRK: σοφία/ sof-ee'-ah): Skilled in insight; imparted dive intelligence. Root: sophistication and philosophy; The art of and affection for wisdom.
dwell (GRK: σκηνώσει/ Skay-no-say): To encamp; tabernacle life; live in intimate communion with Christ as He is with the Father. (Jn 1:14).
Alternate reading: Jn. 4:14 / 7:38 / 3:5; Is. 44:3 / 12:3; Zech. 13:1; Jer. 17:13; I Cor. 10:4).

REFLECTIONS ON REVELATION

THE MULTITUDE OF HEAVEN

Now John sees a great multitude that cannot be counted standing before the Throne of God and worshipping, but in a unique way. This worship makes tribute to Salvation through the Lamb, it is acknowledging an understanding of the redemption process of man by the Messiah. As we can see through study of Matthew 24, there will be a rapture or a taking away of God's people, the Bride of Christ, and it's possible that this scene in Heaven is the great gathering after that; that this group represents the saved from all time. We know that, at the rapture, the dead in Christ will rise first (1 Thes. 4:14-17), and therefore one of the best explanations for this multitude in Heaven is that it is comprised of all saved from throughout history, those who have already passed as well as those who were alive and were raptured with Christ. If this is accurate, then what the congregation of Heaven will do first is identified for us. They go before the throne to worship God and they hold palm branches, which are symbols of victory and of a great arrival (Mat. 21:1-11; Mk. 11:1-11; Lk.19:28-44). John describes them as ones coming out of the Great Tribulation, which probably means the persecution that started at the birth of Christ and lasted throughout church history (Matthew 2:16- 18). However, it could also mean that the Saints of God will spend some time on Earth during the end times Tribulation that we read about in Revelation. They will give their lives for the faith, and since Jesus taught that all who live on Earth will have tribulation (John 16), this could be an example of that teaching. Whoever comprises this congregation in Heaven, we see that they have now escaped the perils that rage on Earth, they have victory over sin, and now are openly in relationship with God. On Earth, during this celebration, the judgements are being loosed as the seals are being broken. The tribulation is in full force and the last, and most grievous seal, the seventh seal, is coming. Find Christ here in the knowledge that while judgement is loosed on Earth, the saints of God will go to the Wedding Supper of the Lamb.

---

1. What is your opinion of this scene in Heaven? Who is there and why?
2. Has the rapture happened here?
3. What do you think of the idea that the tribulation of the church started with the birth of Jesus, and is it different from the tribulation of Revelation?
4. What insights did you gain from the word studies in this session?
5. Share your thoughts and questions from this week's study.

Assigned for next session: (1) Read Revelation chapter eight daily; (2) Journal and record thoughts and questions; (3) Complete session 19 for next class.

NOTES

NOTES

Session 19

FINDING CHRIST IN THE BOOK OF REVELATION

Revelation 8:1-6 (KJV)

SEVENTH SEA AND SILENCE IN HEAVEN

(1) And when he had opened the seventh seal, there was silence in Heaven about the space of half an hour. **(2)** And I saw the seven angels which stood before God; and to them were given seven trumpets. **(3)** And another angel came and stood at the altar, having a golden **censer**; and there was given unto him much incense, that he should offer it with the prayers of all saints upon the golden altar which was before the throne. **(4)** And the smoke of the incense, which came with the prayers of the saints, ascended up before God out of the angel's hand. **(5)** And the angel took the censer, and filled it with fire of the altar, and cast it into the Earth: and there were **voices**, and **thunderings**, and lightnings, and an Earthquake. **(6)** And the seven angels which had the seven trumpets prepared themselves to sound.

---

censer (GRK: λιβανωτός/ lib-an-o-tos'): An Incense Burner with frankincense; frankincense censer.
noises (GRK: φωναὶ/ fo-nai): Rumblings of voices; a voice; a sound; noise; language or dialect.

Reflections on Revelation

THE SEVENTH SEAL AND GOD'S WRATH

As we enter the judgement phase of Revelation and continue to discuss the position of God's holy church during these events, it is a good idea to go back and re-read chapters six through eight. With the seven seals we have seen the initiation of God's wrath towards sin, and along with the coming seven trumpets and seven bowls, they constitute all three sets of judgments listed in Revelation that will occur during the Great Tribulation. The question is, will the church have to endure these judgements, or will the rapture come and rescue the church from the wrath of God? For this study we will present the two main thoughts on this question. There needs to be a distinction made between the persecution of the church that started with the Great Commission and the ascension of Christ, and God's wrath or anger which is loosed on the Earth during the tribulation. The persecution of the church has always been instigated and directed by Satan, but the tribulation is ordered and directed by God. Chapters six through nineteen describe in detail the judgements God will send to the Earth, and if you are a proponent of the post-tribulation rapture, then you believe that this holy judgement will also be residually experienced by the church. The consequences of being here on Earth will be a type of collateral damage suffered by God's children because all on Earth will be exposed to the judgement of God. In this scenario, the persecution of the church is the target and focus of the tribulation, and it supports the idea that the rapture and the second coming are at the end of the tribulation and that they either happen in very close proximity to each other or they are actually the same event. Now those who believe in the pre-tribulation or mid-tribulation rapture see this from a different perspective. As studied in the verses from chapter seven, these interpret the worshipping crowd in Heaven as raptured saints of God mixed with those saved from all time. This theology rests on the idea that the church has authority over Satan because of our association with Christ (Mat. 28), and not only is Jesus' authority with and in the saved by the power of the Holy Spirit, it also rests on the promise that Jesus will never abandon His Church (Deut. 31:6; Heb. 13:5). This seems to support the doctrine of the rapture being an escape from the wrath of the tribulation, and thus it leaves the restoration of Israel as the central focus of Revelation after chapter three is completed and the vision in Heaven begins (Rev. 4). In verse four we see smoke and prayers rising to God with burning incense during a time of total silence; this is not unlike the time of silence and incense held daily in the Temple when the Torah, or the first five books of the Old Testament, was brought in to be read. With the reading of the scroll we see this same pattern of honoring God's Word with silence and contemplation. Now God's judgement is cast to the Earth with fire taken from the altar of God, and this is met by thunder, lightning, voices crying out, and a great earthquake. It is literally Hell on Earth and the world will be shaken to its core. We can find Christ here in a time of silence and prayer honoring the promised Word and acknowledging that God will never leave us or forsake us.

---

1. Why is the fire from the altar of God thrown to the Earth?
2. Share your understanding of when the rapture will happen in proximity to the second coming?
3. What insights did you gain from the word studies in this session?
4. Share your thoughts and questions from this week's study.

Assigned for next session: (1) Read Revelation chapter eight daily; (2) Journal and record thoughts and questions; (3) Complete session 20 for next class.

NOTES

Notes

Session 20

FINDING CHRIST IN THE BOOK OF REVELATION

Revelation 8:7-13 (KJV)

THE FIRST FOUR TRUMPETS

(7) The first angel sounded, and there followed hail and fire mingled with blood, and they were cast upon the Earth: and the third part of trees was burnt up, and all green grass was burnt up. **(8)** And the second angel sounded, and as it were a great mountain burning with fire was cast into the sea: and the third part of the sea became blood; **(9)** And the third part of the creatures which were in the sea, and had life, died; and the third part of the ships were destroyed. **(10)** And the third angel sounded, and there fell a great star from Heaven, burning as it were a lamp, and it fell upon the third part of the rivers, and upon the fountains of waters; **(11)** And the name of the star is called **Wormwood**: and the third part of the waters became wormwood; and many men died of the waters, because they were made bitter. **(12)** And the fourth angel sounded, and the third part of the sun was **smitten**, and the third part of the moon, and the third part of the stars; so as the third part of them was **darkened**, and the day shone not for a third part of it, and the night likewise. **(13)** And I beheld, and heard an angel flying through the midst of Heaven, saying with a loud voice, Woe, woe, woe, to the inhabiters of the Earth by reason of the other voices of the trumpet of the three angels, which are yet to sound!

---

wormwood (GRK: ἄψινθον/ ap'-sin-thon): Oil derived from the most bitter root; a bitter plant; what is intensely bitter (grievous), bringing on very sad results (used only here)

Smitten (GRK: πλήσσω/ place-so): To strike or smite; be deprived of light and shrouded in darkness.

darkened (GRK: σκοτίζω/ skot-id-zo): To darken; to be obscured from God's light; God's depriving of the manifestation of His life (i.e. the sovereign action of God).

Reflections on Revelation

THE ANGELS AND THE TRUMPETS

As the trumpets are sounding, we see great trials loosed on Earth that are very similar to the plagues Moses wrought on Egypt in Exodus chapters seven through eleven. Just as we believe those plagues literally happened, we must also believe that these events will literally happen, in some form or fashion, with the acknowledgement that the literal meaning of the events is unknown. The fourth trumpet seems to be different from the first three, in that it is hard to believe or understand how the Sun, the Moon and the stars can be affected with one third darkened along with a third of the day and night. Many explanations can be discussed for these supernatural events; this darkness could be dust clouds and smoke coming from a great battle, to the point where a third of the suns light is blocked; or, these verses could show God turning his back on Earth and hiding His light. As when He turned his back on Jesus at the cross of sin, therefore he now turns away from the sin held by mankind because of their denial of Christ. This symbol matches the theology that all left on Earth are disgraced by God and lost in sin. If so, this again raises the question, how can the church still be on Earth? A third of the Earth by geographical measure is roughly the size of all the Americas, and in this vast area we see destruction of all the vegetation and waters and no one can eat or drink. Ships are destroyed along with sea life, indicating a natural disaster, not just pollution or poisoning. This event, which is like a great star or meteor falling from the sky, has a name: it is called bitterness and its one purpose is to harm all life on Earth. Finally, we see an angel "flying like an eagle" which could be one of the four beasts which has a head of an eagle, but this is unsubstantiated. Whatever this creature is, it brings a shockingly stern warning that what has been suffered to this point is minimal compared to what is coming. This warning of intensified judgements seems surreal, and is a reminder that today, in this very moment, is the best time for salvation (2 Cor. 6). Find Christ in these verses by knowing He is the champion of the faith and the victor in this war against evil.

---

1. Will the world know what is happening or will there be rampant ignorance?
2. What comparisons can be made to these events and those we read of in the exodus from Egypt?
3. If God does turn his back on of Earth, how can the church still be there?
4. What insights did you gain from the word studies from this session?
5. Share your thoughts and questions from this week's study.

Assigned for next session: (1) Read Revelation chapter nine daily; (2) Journal and record thoughts and questions; (3) Complete session 21 for next class.

Notes

Notes

Session 21

FINDING CHRIST IN THE BOOK OF REVELATION

Revelation 9:1-12 (KJV)

THE FIFTH TRUMPET SOUNDS

(1) And the fifth angel sounded, and I saw a star fall from Heaven unto the Earth: and to him was given the key of the **bottomless pit**. **(2)** And he opened the bottomless pit; and there arose a smoke out of the pit, as the smoke of a great furnace; and the sun and the air were darkened by reason of the smoke of the pit. **(3)** And there came out of the smoke **locusts** upon the Earth: and unto them was given **power**, as the scorpions of the Earth have power. **(4)** And it was commanded them that they should not hurt the grass of the Earth, neither any green thing, neither any tree; but only those men which have not the seal of God in their foreheads. **(5)** And to them it was given that they should not kill them, but that they should be **tormented** five months: and their torment was as the torment of a scorpion, when he striketh a man. **(6)** And in those days shall men seek death, and shall not find it; and shall desire to die, and death shall flee from them. **(7)** And the shapes of the locusts were like unto horses prepared unto battle; and on their heads were as it were crowns like gold, and their faces were as the faces of men. **(8)** And they had hair as the hair of women, and their teeth were as the teeth of lions. **(9)** And they had breastplates, as it were breastplates of iron; and the sound of their wings was as the sound of chariots of many horses running to battle. **(10)** And they had tails like unto scorpions, and there were stings in their tails: and their power was to hurt men five months. **(11)** And they had a king over them, which is the angel of the bottomless pit, whose name in the Hebrew tongue is **Abaddon**, but in the Greek tongue hath his name Apollyon. **(12)** One woe is past; and, behold, there come two woes more hereafter.

---

abyss (GRK: ἀβύσσου/ ab-ess-hou): A boundless abyss with unfathomable depth; home of the dead and evil spirits.
pit (GRK: φρέατος/ phre-atos): A pit; hole; a cistern; a well; an abyss (as a prison).
locusts (GRK: ἀκρίδες/ ak-rei-des): Large flying grasshopper in a numberless swarm).
power (GRK: ἐξουσίαν/ ex-ou-sian): Right and privilege of having power; authority; conferred power; delegated empowerment; authorized to operate in a designated jurisdiction; the authority God gives to act; to be guided by faith (God's revealed word).
torment (GRK:βασανισθήσονται/Bas-an-eis-thes-on-tai): To vex with grievous pain; to examine by torture; to torment or buffet, as of waves; battered; to test (metals) by the touchstone.
Abaddon (GRK: Ἀβαδδών/ ab-add-on): The Destroyer; The Angel of the Abyss; ruin and destruction; one of satanic influence, Satan.

Reflections on Revelation

A GREAT WAR

It seems that the most accurate identification of the force here that is loosed to torment the Earth is Satan. John describes this fallen angel as a fallen star, and writes in the past perfect tense, meaning this angel had already fallen sometime in the past. The star fallen from Heaven and the angel of the abyss can accurately be seen as Satan; and when translating these verses in Greek we read that Abaddon even carries a sub-definition as Satan. This angel is now let loose from the abyss, where Satan fell, and he brings torture, pain, and sorrow. Many interpret the description of the locust as a picture of a modern-day helicopter with missile capabilities like a sting in its tail, with the face of a man, with wings that roar like a rushing chariot, and with a breastplate of iron. The first woe is evil being given power to harm some people, but not all. Remember in chapter seven, the sealed of God from the Twelve Tribes of Israel? Here we see God's provision for them again (v. 5), another example of God using the tribulation to restore Israel unto himself. Where is Christ in this? He can be found in that still small voice that assures us He will keep His promise to sustain those who belong to him. He will not give up.

---

1. See verses seven through twelve; if these are real locusts how can they have a king over them?
2. What are your thoughts about verse six?
3. Who is this fallen angel from verses one and two?
4. What insights did you gain from the word studies from this session?
5. Share your thoughts and questions from this week's study.

Assigned for next session: (1) Read Revelation chapter nine daily; (2) Journal and record thoughts and questions; (3) Complete session 22 for next class.

NOTES

NOTES

SESSION 22

FINDING CHRIST IN THE BOOK OF REVELATION

REVELATION 9:13-21 (KJV)

SIXTH TRUMPET SOUNDS

(13) And the sixth angel sounded, and I heard a voice from the four horns of the golden altar which is before God, **(14)** Saying to the sixth angel which had the trumpet, Loose the four angels which are bound in the great river **Euphrates**. **(15)** And the four angels were loosed, which were prepared for an hour, and a day, and a month, and a year, for to slay the third part of men. **(16)** And the number of the army of the horsemen were two hundred thousand thousand: and I heard the number of them. **(17)** And thus I saw the horses in the vision, and them that sat on them, having breastplates of fire, and of jacinth, and brimstone: and the heads of the horses were as the heads of lions; and out of their mouths issued fire and smoke and brimstone. **(18)** By these three was the third part of men killed, by the fire, and by the smoke, and by the brimstone, which issued out of their mouths. **(19)** For their power is in their mouth, and in their tails: for their tails were like unto serpents, and had heads, and with them they do hurt. **(20)** And the rest of the men which were not killed by these plagues yet repented not of the works of their hands, that they should not worship devils, and idols of gold, and silver, and brass, and stone, and of wood: which neither can see, nor hear, nor walk: **(21)** Neither repented they of their murders, nor of their **sorceries**, nor of their fornication, nor of their thefts.

Euphrates (GRK: Εὐφράτης/ yoo-frat'-ace): The celebrated river that flows from the mountains of Armenia through Assyria, Syria, Mesopotamia and Babylon to the Persian Gulf. (Gen.1:18; Rev.16:12).

sorceries (GRK: φαρμάκων/ Phar-ma-kown): English root-pharmacy; a sorcerer; drug incantations; spells; drugged into living illusions and distortion; Using magical (supernatural) powers to manipulate for gain of temporal possessions or power.

REFLECTIONS ON REVELATION

A GREAT WAR

The sixth trumpet blows and a voice like four horns comes from the golden altar. This symbolism can be compared to the Jewish tradition in the temple that the horns at the altar were a reminder of God's mercy. This altar is the same place that the martyrs ascended to in order to speak to God in chapter eight, and it is now the place of Christ. It represents salvation, grace, and mercy that are driven by judgement and power. The revenge the martyrs asked for is about to be fulfilled. The voice that issues the command to loose the four angels has authority to speak, and that must be God. This scene of justice given to the martyrs from history also shows Christ's fulfilled mission. None that seek God will be forgotten or abandoned; they will be at the center of God's throne. The four angels bound at the Euphrates River could be a reference to the judgements on the influences of Babylon, which is a metaphor for the sin and rebellion of false religions throughout history. The name Babylon means "to be confused", and this connection to humankind's delusion of following themselves is seen here. Remember, Jesus came and was rejected by his own people. At that point even Judaism became a false religion. But the realization of what Babylon represents will bring the sealed of God back to him. In these verses we again see images of what could be compared to modern day war machines. This army of death is very large, and the two-thirds of mankind left on Earth will still refuse to repent of their sin. The judgements will continue because people still seek the power to choose their own path, which is rebellion against God. In verse twenty we see their sin, the worship of idols like the golden calf of the Hebrew Children in Exodus. This desire to pursue the false religion of self is the epitome of what the term Babylon represents. People will choose themselves over the Living God, over love and grace. Sorcery is associated with all types of sin. Throughout Bible history it is connected to the deception of Babylon, to witchcraft, and involves drug use and debauchery. Again, the worship of creation versus the worship of the Creator will seal the fate of many. Truly, humanity without Christ is lost, but we can find Christ today in the power given us through the Spirit of God to see His truth rising in us.

---

1. What are the signs you see today that will bring God's judgement to this world?
2. What is your interpretation of verses 16 through 19?
3. Share examples of deceptions and illusions you see in the world today.
4. What insights did you gain from the word studies in this session?
5. Share your thoughts and questions from this week's study.

Assigned for next session: (1) Read Revelation chapter ten daily; (2) Journal and record thoughts and questions; (3) Complete session 23 for next class.

Notes

Notes

Session 23

FINDING CHRIST IN THE BOOK OF REVELATION

Revelation 10:1-7 (KJV)

THE MIGHTY ANGEL AND THE LITTLE BOOK

(1) And I saw another **mighty** angel come down from Heaven, clothed with a cloud: and a rainbow was upon his head, and his face was as it were the sun, and his feet as pillars of fire: **(2)** And he had in his hand a little book open: and he set his right foot upon the sea, and his left foot on the Earth, (3) And cried with a loud voice, as when a lion roareth: and when he had cried, seven thunders uttered their voices. **(4)** And when the seven thunders had uttered their voices, I was about to write: and I heard a voice from Heaven saying unto me, Seal up those things which the seven thunders uttered, and write them not. **(5)** And the angel which I saw stand upon the sea and upon the Earth lifted up his hand to Heaven, **(6)** And sware by him that **liveth** for ever and ever, who created Heaven, and the things that therein are, and the Earth, and the things that therein are, and the sea, and the things which are therein, that there should be time no longer: **(7)** But in the days of the voice of the seventh angel, when he shall begin to sound, the mystery of God should be finished, as he hath declared to his servants the prophets.

---

mighty (GRK: ἰσχυρὸν/ is-scoo-ron): Strong and powerful; vehement and sure; engaging and combative strength; God's power ready to unleash itself to bring His preferred-will; power through faith; (1 Jn 5:4).

lives (GRK: ζῶντι/ dzown-Tee): To live the God Type of life (From root "Zoe" The God Given Life, different from natural life "Bios"); to be truly alive; To experience God's gift of life from His breath (Gen. 2:7).

Reflections on Revelation

THE PAUSE BEFORE THE FINAL STORM; IT IS FINISHED

The angel written of here has been thought by some to be Christ, which may or may not be true. This angel certainly has Heavenly qualities, coming from Heaven in clouds and with a face shining like the sun. Unlike the angels from the abyss, this angel holds a little book, which translated in Greek means a small papyrus roll or a little scroll. It is an open scroll, and some have called this Ezekiel's scroll, in reference to Ezekiel being told to eat a scroll which was sweet but became bitter in his stomach (Ezekiel 3:1-3). We will discuss more on this in the next session. The cloud reference is comparable to the pillar of cloud that led the children of Israel through the wilderness, which was also a pillar of fire at night (Ex. 13), and also to the transfiguration of Christ and to His ascension. These images seem to represent the delivery of God's Word that saves from being lost and powerless to sin. This angel has a rainbow, like a halo, and some believe this is symbolic of the promise of God to Noah, which is why this angel utters an oath. It is a form of comfort to the reader as it references the promise of God to have mercy on the Earth. This angel does carry God's authority and is speaking God's will but is probably not Jesus himself because in the book of Revelation, John has always identified Christ by name. Here he does not, and this leads many to believe this is a different angel and not Christ. God not allowing John to reveal all that is being said and done is indicative of God withholding certain things from his creation until the appropriate time. This angel sets one foot on the land and one on the sea, representing the entire Earth, and preparing everything for the final woe and God's completed work to be done. Now the identity of the seven thunders or what they say is withheld, but the angel's announcement of no more delays is spoken clearly. These verses seem to mean that at this time God is going to bring time to an end, and that the coming bowl judgements will be the last. God's perfect plan is about to be revealed in a completed work as God has always, and will always, be God. There will be no more mysteries about God or his plan, so look up and get ready: God's going to complete all things. These verses are written with the verb tense of a completed deed that has no end, and though the judgements on the Earth will end, the plan of God for redemption and justice will last forever. This is where we find Christ, in the knowledge that His oaths are always kept.

---

1. Why is God's judgement so necessary?
2. The oath given by the angel to Heaven is significant in what ways?
3. What's the announcement being made by the oath of this angel?
4. What do you think the "Mystery of God" that will be revealed (completed) is? (Acts 1:4-8/ Daniel 12)
5. What insights did you gain from the word studies from this session?
6. Share your thoughts and questions from this week's study.

Assigned for next session: (1) Read Revelation chapter ten daily; (2) Journal and record thoughts and questions; (3) Complete session 24 for next class.

NOTES

Notes

Session 24

FINDING CHRIST IN THE BOOK OF REVELATION

Revelation 10:8-11 (KJV)

THE APOSTLE JOHN EATS THE LITTLE BOOK

(8) And the voice which I heard from Heaven spake unto me again, and said, Go and take the little book which is open in the hand of the angel which standeth upon the sea and upon the Earth. **(9)** And I went unto the angel, and said unto him, Give me the little book. And he said unto me, Take it, and eat it up; and it shall make thy belly **bitter**, but it shall be in thy mouth sweet as honey. **(10)** And I took the little book out of the angel's hand, and ate it up; and it was in my mouth sweet as honey: and as soon as I had eaten it, my belly was bitter. **(11)** And he said unto me, Thou must **prophesy** again before many peoples, and nations, and tongues, and kings.

---

bitter (GRK: πικρανεῖ/ pic-ra-nei): To make bitter; to embitter; To grow angry or harsh.

prophesy (GRK: προφητεῦσαι/ prof-ay-too-sai): To foretell or prophesy; To set forth a matter of divine teaching by special faculty; To speak forth in divinely-empowered forthtelling or foretelling; To reveal the mind (message) of God in a particular situation; Predicting future truth as the Lord reveals.

Reflections on Revelation

THE LITTLE BOOK

John must have been terrified of what he would see next. The little scroll in the angel's hand cannot be the scroll with the seven seals, because only Christ could touch or handle that scroll. But John is literally commanded, "You take, and you eat." He is obedient, but likely quite hesitant to just walk up to this powerful being from the realm of God and take anything, and with the disturbing nature of this vision we can assume John had many reservations. Remember that in many ways this is a new Jesus to John, this is a different relationship than the earthly one he previously had with Christ. We can compare this part of scripture to the prophetic scripture found in the Old Testament when the Prophet Ezekiel was commanded to eat the scroll (Ezekiel 2-3), and assume this coming prophesy is a reference to the House of Israel. Remember that many feel this part of Revelation deals with the restoration of Israel because they have rejected the Messiah. This prophecy is also going to be about the final judgements towards peoples, nations, tongues and kings, of which Israel is not included. In the next session we will see this is also a command for John to go and speak God's Word at the Temple and to the Israelites, while all other nations are gathered there. The angel just swore an oath to Heaven that God's final judgements have arrived, God's completed work is going to be revealed, and many things again speak to the fact that it is possible the church has been raptured by this point. The question that will raise healthy debate is, to what point in the tribulation have we come? It is clear that these events will involve bitter judgement, and although God's perfect plan is sweet, it is also very difficult for many to accept. Remember that this message is evidence that God's Word is complete and never changing. It has always been true that, to the obedient, God's Word is a shield from sin and destruction, but for the disobedient it will be a personal choice to accept judgement and punishment. This is how Christ both changed the Law and fulfilled the Law, as all will have had the chance to receive Christ, but many will choose to disobey and will openly reject salvation, even with knowledge of the truth. There is evidence in Revelation to argue that the entire world will know who Christ is at this point and will still reject Him. It also seems possible that the world will still be ignorant to the truth because of the great deceiver whose power is overtaking the Earth. Regardless, the Antichrist will be their chosen savior, and as we will study later, he and his prophets will deceive those on Earth. They will choose evil over righteousness, arrogance over humility, and sin over holiness. Today we can find Christ in the grace he offers us to deny this kind of fate and to live in the transforming power of His love.

---

1. What is the meaning of God's Word being sweet on the tongue but bitter in the stomach?
2. What are different kinds of prophecies and who is allowed to prophesy?
3. At this point, is there still a chance to be saved during the Great Tribulation? (Rev 7:4 / 20:4)
4. What insights did you gain from the word studies from this session?
5. Share your thoughts and questions from this week's study.

Assigned for next session: (1) Read Revelation chapter eleven daily; (2) Journal and record thoughts and questions; (3) Complete session 25 for next class.

Notes

Notes

SESSION 25

FINDING CHRIST IN THE BOOK OF REVELATION

REVELATION 11:1-6 (KJV)

THE TWO WITNESSES

(1) And there was given me a reed like unto a **rod**: and the angel stood, saying, Rise, and measure the temple of God, and the altar, and them that worship therein. **(2)** But the court which is without the temple leave out, and measure it not; for it is given unto the Gentiles: and the holy city shall they tread under foot forty and two months. **(3)** And I will give power unto my two **witnesses**, and they shall prophesy a thousand two hundred and threescore days, clothed in **sackcloth. (4)** These are the two olive trees, and the two candle-sticks standing before the God of the Earth. **(5)** And if any man will hurt them, fire proceedeth out of their mouth, and devoureth their enemies: and if any man will hurt them, he must in this manner be killed. **(6)** These have power to shut Heaven, that it rain not in the days of their prophecy: and have power over waters to turn them to blood, and to smite the Earth with all plagues, as often as they will.

measuring rod (GRK: κάλαμος / kal'-am-os): A reed or a reed pen; a reed-staff; a measuring rod. (the same word as the scepter given to Jesus with the crown of thorns at His crucifixion, Matthew 27:29).

witnesses (GRK: μάρτυσίν/ mar-ty-syn): A witness; an eye- or ear-witness; a martyr, record, witness; One who is mindful, heeds.

sackcloth: (GRK: σάκκος / sak'-kos): Sackcloth; a sign of mourning; a dArk coarse garment made especially of the hair of animals; Mohair, or the material or garments made of it, worn as a sign of grief.

REFLECTIONS ON REVELATION

GOD'S WITNESS TO ISRAEL

The inner court mentioned here, and its inhabitants, is probably a reference to the lost nation of Israel. We again see a distinction between Israel and the rest of the world; and since God would never exclude the church from the inner court, this also could be seen as evidence that by this point the church has been raptured. (Revelation 5 and 6). The remaining time of Revelation seems to be assigned to discuss the restoration of Israel as prophesied by the Apostle Paul (Romans 11:25-29 and to the judgements of God towards a rebellious Earth. God's Word never identifies the saved as anyone but those who have accepted Christ, so these verses point towards God's desire for Israel to accept Christ as their Messiah and to join the saved of God. In chapter five we saw the church, comprised of the saints of God, in the throne room of Heaven worshipping God. Here we see the Gentiles excluded from the inner court; this must point to the lost souls of the Gentiles still inhabiting the Earth and is not a reference to the Christian Gentiles whom God has already accepted unto Himself. Regardless of when during the tribulation this all happens, we know that both of these purposes, for God to save the church and to save Israel, will take place. The three and one-half years is seen by many to mean either the start of or the latter half of the tribulation. Now, there are several schools of thought as to who the two witnesses are, but what they represent and what they preach are more important than who they are. The two lampstands and olive trees are symbols of the giving of light, life, and power. Olive oil was commonly burned in lamps of that day and we know that the lampstand is representative of the church (Rev. 1). It seems that these messengers will prophesy the truth of God's church, the rejection of Jesus the true Messiah, and will call for repentance from the House of Israel. Some believe these two are Biblical patriarchs who have come back to Earth to proclaim God's Message, like Moses, Elijah, John the Baptist, or Enoch. God's word does not tell us who they are, only that they will stand before the "God of the Earth" and prophesy. They will, for a time, have complete power to do as they will, but the lost and sinful world, or the outer court, will be directed by the spirit of Antichrist to oppose them. Satan's hatred will grow, and the Earth will become a united warring power bent on defeating God. At this point the only connection of God to the Earth seems to be the Nation of Israel. We can find Christ in our personal knowledge that we have found the truth and we can enter the Holy of Holies at any point, on our knees, and speak with the living God.

1. Why do you think John is told to measure the area of the temple set aside for the chosen people?
2. Why do the two witnesses wear sackcloth, a sign of mourning?
3. What insights did you gain from the word studies from this session?
4. Share your thoughts and questions from this week's study.

Assigned for next session: (1) Read Revelation chapter eleven daily; (2) Journal and record thoughts and questions; (3) Complete session 26 for next class.

Notes

NOTES

SESSION 26

FINDING CHRIST IN THE BOOK OF REVELATION

REVELATION 11:7-14 (KJV)

THE WITNESSES KILLED, THEN RESURRECTED

(7) And when they shall have finished their testimony, the **beast** that ascendeth out of the bottomless pit shall make war against them, and shall overcome them, and kill them. **(8)** And their dead bodies shall lie in the street of the great city, which spiritually is called Sodom and Egypt, where also our Lord was crucified. **(9)** And they of the people and kindreds and tongues and nations shall see their dead bodies three days and an half, and shall not suffer their dead bodies to be put in graves. **(10)** And they that dwell upon the Earth shall rejoice over them, and **make merry**, and shall send gifts one to another; because these two prophets **tormented** them that dwelt on the Earth. **(11)** And after three days and an half the **spirit of life** from God entered into them, and they stood upon their feet; and great fear fell upon them which saw them. **(12)** And they heard a great voice from Heaven saying unto them, Come up hither. And they ascended up to Heaven in a cloud; and their enemies beheld them. **(13)** And the same hour was there a great Earthquake, and the tenth part of the city fell, and in the Earthquake were slain of men seven thousand: and the remnant were affrighted, and gave glory to the God of Heaven. **(14)** The second woe is past; and, behold, the third woe cometh quickly.

---

beast (GRK: θηρίον/ They-rion): A wild animal or brut; generic-wild animal; having a brutal or bestial nature.
make merry (GRK: εὐφραίνονται/ Eu-phrain-on-tai): To cheer or revel and feast; a merry outlook; a cheery mind because of feeling the sense of victory ("inner triumph").
tormented (GRK: ἐβασάνισαν/ eb-bas-on-I-son): To examine with torture or torment; To buffet like waves of the seashore; to test (metals) by the touchstone; to vex with grievous pains; to be harassed, distressed.
Spirit of Life (GRK: πνεῦμα / pneu-mah): Spirit wind; breath of God that animates life; Spirit of life from God.

REFLECTIONS ON REVELATION

GOD'S POWER ON DISPLAY

God's witnesses have finished their task to deliver the message of God to the world, and it is revealing that the world perceives them as tormentors and evil; they hate them. Many forces in the world today already carry this spirit of Antichrist. They deem God's Word a delusion and believe that humanistic pursuits are the only real path to truth. Make no mistake, Christianity is already on trial in this world. At this point in Revelation the world's powers, who had tried and failed to destroy God's voice, have finally found a miraculous power to oppose God. This power, the beast, is allowed to rise from the pit of Hell and, for a time, destroy the witnesses of God and deceive those of the Earth. The name used here in Greek for the beast is used throughout the rest of Revelation to signify the one in opposition to Jesus Christ. It is easy to see the contrast between this beast who brings death, and Christ, the Lamb, who brings life (John 8:44; John 14:6). There are many beasts mentioned in Revelation, and some have questioned which beast this is, but most scholars agree this is probably the true Antichrist. Whatever position you take we know that the world's deluded inhabitants will follow these false deliverers, and they will receive this being as if he were the messiah. He will seem to have supernatural power to save and will be a mirror image of Jesus but will have evil intent, and eventually will be proven powerless. The entire new world order will fall for this deception and will follow God's plan while being deceived into thinking that they are following their own plans. They will celebrate death, but the celebration will be short lived. Only three short days and God will bring the entire world back to the reality that you cannot escape His Word. These verses seem to take us into a new vision of the world, which is now seen fully as the fallen kingdom, and with this we now have a new name for the capitol of sin and rebellion: Jerusalem, now called Sodom and Egypt. These two Biblical places, where the domain of sin and bondage reigned, now reveal the world's addiction to sin. In all of literature there has never been a more revealing picture of sin than here. The city Jesus once wept over is now representative of humankind's rebellion against God and will be utterly destroyed. We find Jesus here, at the cross, asking and pleading for all to come to Him, before it's too late.

---

1. Discuss human arrogance. Where do we see it in this world today?
2. What is the significance of the witnesses being dead three days?
3. How is Christianity already on trial in this world?
4. What insights did you gain from the word studies from this session?
5. Share your thoughts and questions from this week's study.

Assigned for next session: (1) Read Revelation chapter eleven daily; (2) Journal and record thoughts and questions; (3) Complete session 27 for next class.

Notes

NOTES

Session 27

FINDING CHRIST IN THE BOOK OF REVELATION

Revelation 11:15-19 (KJV)

SEVENTH TRUMPET: THE KINGDOM PROCLAIMED

(15) And the seventh angel sounded; and there were great voices in Heaven, saying, The kingdoms of this world are become the kingdoms of our Lord, and of his **Christ**; and he shall reign for ever and ever. **(16)** And the four and twenty elders, which sat before God on their seats, fell upon their faces, and worshipped God, **(17)** Saying, We give thee thanks, O Lord God **Almighty**, which art, and wast, and art to come; because thou hast taken to thee thy great power, and hast **reigned**. **(18)** And the nations were angry, and thy wrath is come, and the time of the dead, that they should be judged, and that thou shouldest give reward unto thy servants the prophets, and to the saints, and them that fear thy name, small and great; and shouldest destroy them which destroy the Earth. **(19)** And the temple of God was opened in Heaven, and there was seen in his temple the Ark of his testament: and there were lightnings, and voices, and thunderings, and an Earthquake, and great hail.

Christ (GRK: Χριστοῦ/ Kri-stou): The Anointed One; in Hebrew, Messiah.
almighty (GRK: Παντοκράτωρ/ Pan-to-cra-tor): Almighty Ruler of the universe; unrestricted power to exercising absolute dominion.
reigned (GRK: ἐβασίλευσας/ ay-bas-ill-eu-sas): To be king; exercise kingly power, the highest influence.

Reflections on Revelation

JESUS IS KING OF ALL THE EARTH

The seventh trumpet sounds, and many feel that this is the announcement of the second coming of Christ and the great battle. One reason is that in these verses we see the Ark of the Covenant before God. The Israelite people were always commanded to take the Ark into battle to ensure victory. The Ark of Moses and the Ten Commandments disappeared in 600 BC when Babylon destroyed the temple. In the second temple period, during the time of Jesus, there is no mention of the Ark. Well, now we know where it was all this time, and it has been preserved for the final and most intense battle. If this is the great and final battle to conquer sin and restore Israel to God, then it makes sense that the Ark would be there. This third woe is the announcement that will bring all the Earth back to reality, and this event is met with worship and thanksgiving before the throne of God as his power is being loosed and all in Heaven know to bow down. Remember earlier we saw John being told to keep certain events secret until the correct time? Well, now we are allowed to see the coming purpose of God very clearly. The language used here in the Greek is unmistakable. It is written in what is called an ingressive aorist tense. This denotes a state of continuing action and it expresses the beginning, or entrance into, a new state of being. Adam and Eve were given dominion on Earth at creation, but they traded that authority to Satan at the fall of man for a piece of fruit. Since then, Satan has had the right to certain God-given authority, and this is why the Bible calls him the ruler of this world (John 12:31). He has deceived God's creation into not wanting to be governed by God even when they can see Him clearly. Now, when they see the truth and the reality of their sin, they become angry. Judgement has not influenced them to humility or repentance, only into deeper hate and rebellion. Verse eighteen mentions the dead, and it carries with it an emphasis on righteous vengeance. This could mean that the time when we see God's judgement for the martyring of the saints of God has come, and the promise of God from chapter six is now fulfilled. All those who followed evil and sin, both in the past and present, now seem to be put on notice that all the injustices of history will now be made right. The lightnings, rumblings, and thunder have been associated with the coming bowl judgements, and the forces of evil that deceived the Earth will also be under judgement now. We can find Christ in these verses by knowing that all who can be saved will be saved by a loving God.

---

1. What causes some people to miss God's love and grace? (2 Cor. 4:1-6)
2. After all we have seen happening in Revelation, how could there still be rebellion?
3. Why are we shown the Ark of the Covenant in these verses?
4. What insights did you gain from the word studies from this session?
5. Share your thoughts and questions from this week's study.

Assigned for next session: (1) Read Revelation chapter twelve daily; (2) Journal and record thoughts and questions; (3) Complete session 28 for next class.

Notes

NOTES

SESSION 28

FINDING CHRIST IN THE BOOK OF REVELATION

REVELATION 12:1-6 (KJV)

THE WOMAN, THE CHILD, AND THE DRAGON

(1) And there appeared a **great wonder** in Heaven; a woman clothed with the sun, and the moon under her feet, and upon her head a **crown** of twelve stars: **(2)** And she being with child cried, travailing in birth, and pained to be delivered. **(3)** And there **appeared** another wonder in Heaven; and behold a great red **dragon**, having seven heads and ten horns, and seven **crowns** upon his heads. **(4)** And his tail drew the third part of the stars of Heaven, and did cast them to the Earth: and the dragon stood before the woman which was ready to be delivered, for to devour her child as soon as it was born. **(5)** And she brought forth a man child, who was to rule all nations with a rod of iron: and her child was caught up unto God, and to his throne. **(6)** And the woman fled into the wilderness, where she hath a place prepared of God, that they should feed her there a thousand two hundred and threescore days.

---

great wonder (GRK: σημεῖον/ Sei-Mei-On): A sign; a miracle; an indication; a mark or token.
crown (GRK: στέφανος/stef-a-nos): A surrounding garland of honor and glory. The crown of victory; the eternal blessedness which will be given as a prize to the genuine servants of God.
appeared (lit-was seen) (GRK: ὤφθη/ Oph-they): To see with the eyes: to see with the mind, to perceive, know: observe, give attention to.
dragon (GRK: δράκων / drak-own): A mythical huge serpent; Satan; exercising subtle, indirect impact on heathen governments; accomplishing Hellish agendas from behind the scenes. Having incredible insight, able to spot prey in any hiding place.
Crowns (GRK: διαδήματα/ dia-dem-ata): A diadem; a royal crown; a head-wreath; kingly ornament for the head; the end-times coalition led by Antichrist against the infinite majesty and kingship of Christ (Rev 19:12).

REFLECTIONS ON REVELATION

THE BATTLE LINES HAVE BEEN DRAWN

There are many theologically sound ways of viewing these verses; those who consider Jesus' earthly mother as holy deity, but not in the sense of being part of the Trinity, see this woman as literally the Virgin Mary. She is seen as the matriarch of the entire existence of mankind through her association with the saving Christ. Others have identified this woman as the nation of Israel whom Jesus is seeking to restore unto Himself. Their association with Christ has made them an enemy of Satan (Ezekiel 16; Genesis 37); and in this scenario the twelve stars represent the tribes of Israel. These verses are written in the perfect verb tense, representing a completed action that has always been. This action is the continual covering and protection from God to this woman. Those who support post-tribulation rapture see this woman as possibly the modern-day Christian Church, like the bride of Christ (John 3:29; Matt. 9:15; Mark 2:19). Now, before you dismiss this, remember that the church is characterized as ten virgins in Matthew 25 and is called "the Israel of God" in Galatians 6:16; this term in modern interpretation is commonly seen as the holy church. It is possible with these scenarios that all saved from throughout history are included in this vision as part of the woman, but realistically, the true and complete meaning of the identity of the woman is a mystery. We know she has a place with God and is going to be part of this battle between good and evil. Now the Child is obviously Jesus Christ, as only He could fulfill the criteria listed in verse five. Only Jesus, who was with God at creation and then came to Earth as man, can be a direct descendant and a previous ancestor of the woman. He has a special relationship to the woman and this flashback to the birth of Christ is a reminder of the plan of God to crush the serpent's head, as seen in Genesis chapter three. What we know for sure is that the dragon is Satan, the two beasts are the Antichrist and his prophet, and the seven heads, ten horns, and the seven diadems are some combination of nations, governments, and military powers of the Earth. These beings and entities will comprise the enemies of God during the final battle after the tribulation. This picture is of grace and mercy extended to all on Earth from God throughout the tribulation. This is where Christ is found in these verses, in God's plan to save, to overcome evil and sin, and to offer reconciliation to all who will accept Him.

---

1. Who do you think the woman is?
2. Who are the seven heads, diadems, or ten horns?
3. What insights did you gain from the word studies from this session?
4. Share your thoughts and questions from this week's study.

Assigned for next session: (1) Read Revelation chapter twelve daily; (2) Journal and record thoughts and questions; (3) Complete session 29 for next class.

NOTES

Notes

Session 29

FINDING CHRIST IN THE BOOK OF REVELATION

Revelation 12:7-12 (KJV)

SATAN THROWN OUT OF HEAVEN

(7) And there was war in Heaven: **Michael** and his angels fought against the dragon; and the dragon fought and his angels, **(8)** And prevailed not; neither was their place found any more in Heaven. **(9)** And the great dragon was cast out, that old serpent, called the **Devil**, and Satan, which deceiveth the whole world: he was cast out into the Earth, and his angels were cast out with him. **(10)** And I heard a loud voice saying in Heaven, Now is come **salvation**, and strength, and the kingdom of our God, and the power of his Christ: for the accuser of our **brethren** is cast down, which **accused** them before our God day and night. **(11)** And they overcame him by the blood of the Lamb, and by the word of their testimony; and they loved not their lives unto the death. **(12)** Therefore rejoice, ye Heavens, and ye that dwell in them. Woe to the inhabiters of the Earth and of the sea! for the devil is come down unto you, having great wrath, because he knoweth that he hath but a short time.

Michael (GRK: ἀρχάγγελος / Ark-an-gel-lous): The Chief Angel or archangel. (1 Thes. 4:16; Jude 9; Dan 10:13; Dan 12:1).
devil (GRK: Διάβολος/ di-ab-o-los): The slanderous; a false accuser; unjustly criticizing to hurt; to malign and condemn; to sever a relationship; backbiter.
salvation (GRK: σωτηρία/ so-ter-iyah): Deliverance to save; welfare, prosperity; preservation; safety; God's rescue out of destruction and into His safety.
brethren (GRK: ἀδελφῶν/ a-del-phone): Members of the same religious community; a fellow-Christian; A brother from the same womb; brothers by blood.
accuser (GRK: κατήγωρ/ kate-gor): A prosecutor; plaintiff in the assembly of law; Satan, who makes charge against and prosecutes God's chosen.

Reflections on Revelation

FREE FROM ACCUSATIONS

Michael is identified in Daniel as a powerful archangel who is one of the protectors of God's people (Dan. 10 and 12). This mighty warrior is seen here assisting God in defending Heaven at the time when Satan's ability to accuse God's children was taken away. It is not clear why Satan was ever able to petition God to accuse the saints, but at this point his voice is shut up. We see Satan and his factions of demons and fallen angels cast out of all connection to God, and symbolically cast to the Earth or the place of sin. When banished to Earth, Satan goes with hate and fury and the Earth pays the price for this. Just imagine what the members of the churches of that day, who were reading these letters, had seen up to that moment in their existence. They had seen Satan's wrath on Earth perpetrated towards them. What can be worse than the evil that has already been experienced throughout their history? Yet when the tribulation starts there will be unprecedented evil released on this Earth. In this message God is again giving hope for a victorious future. The Blood of the Lamb which covers all sin, and the power of choosing to walk with Christ in a dark world, makes Satan's accusations against sinners no longer valid. This is a confirmation to the church that no matter what happens in this world, no one on Earth or in Heaven can ever accuse them again. In God's court, all of his children are seen as innocent. Some believe that this is a view of what happened in Heaven, either when Christ was born, when he was crucified, or when he was resurrected. Regardless of what events surround this vision, we see that these verses are an invitation to come alongside of God in his holy purpose to reach the world with salvation. It is a reassurance that there is an unimaginably blessed future that awaits all who believe. The churches of that day would have understood this in a very personal way, and God was reinforcing in their minds, and now in ours, that the eternal destiny that motivates their choices will be worth every sacrifice. Find Christ today in the knowledge that he has given us more than we can ever deserve.

---

1. How can anyone be innocent before God?
2. Why did God allow Satan to speak to accuse believers before His throne? (Job 1:1-12)
3. What does verse eleven mean to you?
4. What insights did you gain from the word studies from this session?
5. Share your thoughts and questions from this week's study.

Assigned for next session: (1) Read Revelation chapter twelve daily; (2) Journal and record thoughts and questions; (3) Complete session 30 for next class.

NOTES

Notes

Session 30

FINDING CHRIST IN THE BOOK OF REVELATION

Revelation 12:13-17 (KJV)

THE WOMAN PERSECUTED

(13) And when the dragon saw that he was **cast** unto the Earth, he **persecuted** the woman which brought forth the man child. **(14)** And to the woman were given two wings of a great eagle, that she might fly into the wilderness, into her place, where she is **nourished** for a time, and times, and half a time, from the **face** of the serpent. **(15)** And the serpent cast out of his mouth water as a flood after the woman, that he might cause her to be carried away of the flood. **(16)** And the Earth helped the woman, and the Earth opened her mouth, and swallowed up the flood which the dragon cast out of his mouth. **(17)** And the dragon was wroth with the woman, and went to make war with the remnant of her seed, which keep the commandments of God, and have the testimony of Jesus Christ.

---

cast (GRK: ἐβλήθη / e-bleth-ay): To throw away from; To place or drop with force and effort; violently displaced from a position gained.
Persecuted (GRK: ἐδίωξεν / edi-oxen): To put to flight, to pursue, to hunt down.
Nourished (feminine) (GRK: τρέφεται/ treph-et-ai): Make to grow; feed; To bring up or rear; provide for; fully develop and adequately nourished; experience spiritual development; properly fed; nursed and fattened to health.
Face Of (GRK: προσώπου / pros-o-pou): The presence of; faced with accusations; countenance; surface of a face; see the appearance of; in the presence of; to stand against, resist, withstand.

Reflections on Revelation

ISRAEL WILL NEVER BE ABANDONED

In the drama that is Revelation chapter twelve we have three main characters. The woman, the Child, and the dragon. The Child, we know, is Jesus Christ, the Messiah. The dragon is Satan, which was established previously in these studies; and so we are left to consider who the woman is. Redemption and deliverance are, in part, the themes of these verses, and many argue that any of the events surrounding the crucifixion, the resurrection, or the day of Pentecost (Acts 2) could be described here. But, before you finalize those thoughts, could this not also be a description of the entirety of the plan of God to defeat Satan, and these characters examples of the struggle between God and evil throughout history? This formula could include everything from creation to the tribulation and beyond. This could also include the Israelites' flight out of Egypt, which would explain the twelve stars on the woman's crown being the Twelve Tribes of Israel. This flight and rescue on eagle's wings has been seen as part of the Old Testament tradition of symbolically describing God's deliverance for Israel (Isaiah 40:31; Exodus 19:4). We know that it is part of God's plan to bring Israel back into connection with their long-awaited Messiah, and if this is the rebirth of redemption for Israel it would support the view that, at this point, the church has already been taken from the Earth. Regardless of which path you chose to take; the purpose of these verses is to emphasize the plan of God to redeem a chosen group of people of Earth that he has sealed unto Himself. Even now God's grace and deliverance can be seen with the escape route of the woman, and since we know from recent sessions that all redeemed by Christ have already been delivered from Satan's ability to accuse them, how can this group, who must escape Satan, be the Christian Church? And remember, the redeemed of God have the promise to escape the wrath to come (I Thess. 1:10; Rom 5:9-10). The theme of these verses seems to include deliverance and spiritual renewal, and if the redeemed of God are born again, then who will God need to protect, but the chosen ones of Israel? And if this is true, then these verses describe a nation that has come to its senses and seen Christ as the Messiah. Can you imagine any group of people that Satan would hate more? Whoever is still on Earth and under God's protection at this point will be sought by Satan, and since Satan cannot now accuse the saints of God, who else could these people be?

---

1. What do you make of these verses, and what events do they represent?
2. Who could need redemption at this point, if this is all happening in the tribulation?
3. What insights did you gain from the word studies from this session?
4. Share your thoughts and questions from this week's study

Assigned for next session: (1) Read Revelation chapter thirteen daily; (2) Journal and record thoughts and questions; (3) Complete session 31 for next class.

Notes

NOTES

Session 31

FINDING CHRIST IN THE BOOK OF REVELATION

Revelation 13:1-10 (KJV)

THE BEAST FROM THE SEA

(1) And I stood upon the sand of the sea, and saw a beast rise up out of the sea, having seven heads and ten horns, and upon his horns ten crowns, and upon his heads the name of blasphemy. **(2)** And the beast which I saw was like unto a leopard, and his feet were as the feet of a bear, and his mouth as the mouth of a lion: and the dragon gave him his power, and his seat, and great authority. **(3)** And I saw one of his heads as it were **wounded to death**; and his deadly wound was healed: and all the world wondered after the beast. **(4)** And they worshipped the dragon which gave power unto the beast: and they worshipped the beast, saying, Who is like unto the beast? who is able to make war with him? **(5)** And there was given unto him a mouth speaking great things and blasphemies; and **power** was given unto him to continue forty and two months. **(6)** And he opened his mouth in blasphemy against God, to blaspheme his name, and his tabernacle, and them that dwell in Heaven. **(7)** And it was given unto him to make war with the saints, and to overcome them: and power was given him over all kindreds, and tongues, and nations. **(8)** And all that dwell upon the Earth shall worship him, whose names are not written in the book of life of the Lamb slain from the foundation of the world. **(9)** If any man have an ear, let him hear. **(10)** He that leadeth into captivity shall go into captivity: he that killeth with the sword must be killed with the sword. Here is the patience and the faith of the saints.

---

power (GRK: ἐξουσίαν/ Ex-ou-si-an): Authority to act; weight; moral authority and influence; spiritual power in the Earth. (For further understanding see Daniel Chapter 7).

wounded (GRK: σφάζω / sfad'-zo): Slay or slaughter; kill by violence; wound mortally; To butcher or put to death by violence.

Reflections on Revelation

THE FOUR BEASTS OF DANIEL AND REVELATION

In Daniel chapter seven we see four beasts identified, and we have now seen two beasts in Revelation. Are these beasts the same beings or do they reveal a discrepancy in the scriptures? Many argue for or against these books being records of the same prophesy, but in this study, we will lean towards accepting them as being connected and trust the Holy Spirit to guide us through their interpretations. This beast rises from the sea and comes to aid Satan in his deception of the world. He has a slightly different description than in Revelation chapter eleven but is still evil and satanic in nature. He is connected to the dragon, whom we know is Satan, and their deceptions together will bring the world to the end of grace. Those caught in this deception will join Satan in persecuting those who have discovered the truth. Now there are three views of who these saints from verse seven might be. Many see these saints as the un-raptured church, and if this is true, then this would support a mid- or post-tribulation rapture. A very popular belief is that there will be unsaved Gentiles, after the rapture, who were left behind only to realize the truth and, through a martyr's death, achieve salvation. The third view is again attributed to the restoration of the nation of Israel, with these now Messianic Jews finding the truth of Christ. Whichever path you support, we know Satan will be given power to wreak havoc on the Earth and attack those of the faith. He then blasphemes and mocks God as he imitates the crucifixion and resurrection with the mortal wounding and miraculous recovery of one of the seven heads (v. three). With this, all those left on Earth will be deceived and no one will have power to resist the possession of their minds (2 Thessalonians 2:9; Romans 1:18-32; 2 Timothy 3:1-5). Many believe, with the mention of the Lamb's Book of Life, that verse eight symbolizes the end of grace. It would therefore also be the end of the Great Commission, and all that will be left is judgement and correction brought by the evil power loaned to Satan by God. Finding faith in a lost world is the key to finding Christ in these verses, as until the Lamb's Book of Life is closed, all have the opportunity to choose eternal life with God.

---

1. What do all of these events from Daniel, Ezekiel, and Revelation mean to you?
2. Who are the saints in verse seven?
3. Is grace going to end someday; if so, when will this happen?
4. What insights did you gain from the word studies from this session?
5. Share your thoughts and questions from this week's study

Assigned for next session: (1) Read Revelation chapter thirteen daily; (2) Journal and record thoughts and questions; (3) Complete session 32 for next class.

NOTES

Notes

Session 32

FINDING CHRIST IN THE BOOK OF REVELATION

Revelation 13:11-18 (KJV)

THE BEAST FROM THE EARTH

(11) And I beheld **another** beast coming up out of the Earth; and he had two horns like a lamb, and he spake as a dragon. **(12)** And he **exerciseth** all the power of the first beast before him, and **causeth** the Earth and them which dwell therein to worship the first beast, whose **deadly wound** was healed. **(13)** And he doeth great wonders, so that he maketh fire come down from Heaven on the Earth in the sight of men, **(14)** And deceiveth them that dwell on the Earth by the means of those miracles which he had power to do in the sight of the beast; saying to them that dwell on the Earth, that they should make an image to the beast, which had the wound by a sword, and did live. **(15)** And he had power to give life unto the image of the beast, that the image of the beast should both speak, and cause that as many as would not worship the image of the beast should be killed. **(16)** And he causeth all, both small and great, rich and poor, free and bond, to receive a **mark** in their right hand, or in their foreheads: **(17)** And that no man might buy or sell, save he that had the mark, or the name of the beast, or the number of his name. **(18)** Here is wisdom. Let him that hath **understanding** count the **number** of the beast: for it is the number of a man; and his number is Six hundred threescore and six. (666)

---

another (GRK: ἄλλος / al'-los): Another (of more than two); a different one or different from the first.
exercises (GRK: ποιεῖ/ Poi-ay): To produce, construct, or cause in some form or fashion; to make a path; to be operative, exercise activity; To Manufacture.
wounded (GRK: πληγὴν / Play-gen): A blow, wound; To stripe; to cause an affliction or plague.
mark (GRK: χάραγμα/khar'-ag-mah): A stamp or impression; sculpture; engraving; a sign.
understanding (GRK: νοῦν / noun): The mind; understanding and reason; the reasoning faculty or intellect; comprehension; perceiving and understanding and those of feeling, judging, determining.
number (GRK: ἀριθμός/ ar-ith-mos): A number or total; a group of numbers; a calculated total.

Reflections on Revelation

GOD IS NOT MOCKED

In these verses Satan is still manufacturing God-like political and spiritual influences on the nations and peoples of the Earth. The second beast is now introduced to the world. This entity is identified as a "false prophet" (Rev. 19) and, combined with the dragon, or Satan, these two beasts form an un-holy triad of figures mimicking the Holy Trinity. This second beast comes up from the Earth and, with the two horns of authority, starts some sort of political-religious movement. There is not enough evidence given to us to clearly identify what is taking place here, but this power comes from the authority of Earth and connects Satan directly to the world's systems of government, religion, and science. This second beast does not seek acclaim or recognition for himself but directs all glory and honor to the Antichrist, not unlike what John the Baptist did as the prophet preparing the way for Jesus. This movement will force, upon pain of death, all the world's populations to bow and accept the mark of the beast, which we finally see here in verse eighteen, the infamous number 666. We are challenged here to try to discern what the mark of the beast is, and many have tried. In this study I will only include that in ancient Greek, and in Hebrew, numbers are represented by letters, and some have suggested that this number in letter form represents the movement to destroy Christianity at the time. This movement was started by Caesar Nero, and some believe the 666 number means "Caesar Nero." What is sure is that this spirit of persecution that was birthed by Satan when Jesus was born has survived within humankind throughout the history of the church, and you can see this hatred for God alive in the world today. Remember that, although this evil mentality is alive today, all who encounter the Spirit of God can still find Christ and the truth in these, the end times. (I Thessalonians 5).

---

1. What are your thoughts on Revelation 13?
2. Why does Satan present himself to be like God?
3. What are your thoughts of the mark of the beast? (Rev 13:16)
4. What insights did you gain from the word studies from this session?
5. Share your thoughts and questions from this week's study.

Assigned for next session: (1) Read Revelation chapter fourteen daily; (2) Journal and record thoughts and questions; (3) Complete session 33 for next class.

Notes

NOTES

SESSION 33

FINDING CHRIST IN THE BOOK OF REVELATION

REVELATION 14:1-5 (KJV)

THE HOLY ARMY OF GOD

(1) And I looked, and, lo, a Lamb stood on the mount **Sion**, and with him an hundred forty and four thousand, having his **Father's** name written in their foreheads. **(2)** And I heard a voice from Heaven, as the voice of many waters, and as the voice of a great thunder: and I heard the voice of harpers harping with their harps: **(3)** And they sung as it were a new song before the throne, and before the four beasts, and the elders: and no man could learn that song but the hundred and forty and four thousand, which were redeemed from the Earth. **(4)** These are they which were not **defiled** with women; for they are virgins. These are they which follow the Lamb whithersoever he goeth. These were redeemed from among men, being the firstfruits unto God and to the Lamb. **(5)** And in their mouth was found no guile: for they are without fault before the throne of God.

---

sion (GRK: Σιών/ see-own): Zion; The mountain top that is part of the Old City of Jerusalem; The place where God spared Abraham's son Isaac, and then gave his own Son Jesus; the name used to describe Jerusalem and/or God's Throne.

father (GRK: πατήρ / pat-ayr): A Heavenly ancestor; elder or senior; one who imparts and is committed to life; a progenitor; the giver of eternal life through the second birth; Giver of ongoing sanctification.

defile (GRK: μολύνω / mol-oo-no): To stain or defile; to pollute; to make mucky (dirty); To become spiritually soiled; sin smearing with spiritual filth; moral soil or smut that befouls and soils (Aristotle and Plato).

REFLECTIONS ON REVELATION

HEAVEN AND EARTH COMING TOGETHER

John's vision here shows Jesus, on Earth, standing on or near Mount Zion in Jerusalem. This is where King David dwelled, where Solomon built the first Temple which encompassed God's Dwelling in the Holy of Holies, and is near to Calvary, where Jesus was crucified. It is possible that these verses paint a picture of the millennial kingdom to come, in which the masses surrounding God's throne are the saints of Heaven from all time, which would include the raptured church. This view would also see the 144,000 with Christ as the "sealed of God" mentioned in Revelation chapter seven. In this millennial kingdom, we see a picture of God's throne, sometimes called Mount Sion, united with Christ's throne on Earth, sometimes called Mount Zion. The theme of this new vision would be different from previous views of God's throne in the Bible. Those views were centered in the work of grace and the redemption of man, while this new vision is centered around the completed work of God, which would include the restoration of Israel unto their Messiah (Ps. 91:1-16; Ruth 2:12; Jer. 29:11; Is 40:31). We can justify seeing those with Christ as the same sealed of God that were identified in chapter seven, as they have seen and accepted the truth about Jesus Christ, and they are again called the sealed of God. They follow Jesus wherever He goes, they are called the first fruits of the harvest, which is traditional title for the children of Israel, and they have a supernatural covering that has given them a special place because of their immunity to human desires. This spiritual and moral purity, which also includes power to control the tongue, (1 Pet. 3:10; Eph. 4:29; Jam. 3:1-12), has made them overcomers like no other Christians in history. We know they are sinners saved by grace since they are called "redeemed," but they are chosen to follow Christ into the final battle with Satan (Gal. 5:19-21). To focus on who these people are or where this all takes place would be to miss the most important point of this chapter, which is to reveal that God's holy plan will be completed. For all Christians today, they can find Christ here in the knowledge that all who are covered with His grace are seen as innocent though they were formerly sinners, and that they are part of the completed work of God.

---

1. What is the message of these verses in Revelation?
2. Where is Jesus in this vision, and why is Mt. Zion part of this vision? (Revelations 11:15-19)
3. If sin defiles, and God provides sanctification from sin through Christ, then what is a person's duty and task in this process towards sanctification? (2 Thess. 2:13-14; Gal. 5:22-23; I Cor. 12:12-14; 1 Pet. 4:1-2)
4. What insights did you gain from the word studies from this session?
5. Share your thoughts and questions from this week's study.

Assigned for next session: (1) Read Revelation chapter fourteen daily; (2) Journal and record thoughts and questions; (3) Complete session 34 for next class.

Notes

Notes

Session 34

FINDING CHRIST IN THE BOOK OF REVELATION

Revelation 14:6-13 (KJV)

THE PROCLAMATIONS OF THREE ANGELS

(6) And I saw another angel fly in the midst of Heaven, having the **everlasting gospel** to preach unto them that dwell on the Earth, and to every nation, and kindred, and tongue, and people, **(7)** Saying with a loud voice, Fear God, and give glory to him; for the hour of his judgment is come: and worship him that made Heaven, and Earth, and the sea, and the fountains of waters. **(8)** And there followed another angel, saying, **Babylon** is fallen, is fallen, that great city, because she made all nations drink of the wine of the wrath of her **fornication**. **(9)** And the third angel followed them, saying with a loud voice, If any man worship the beast and his image, and receive his mark in his forehead, or in his hand, **(10)** The same shall drink of the wine of the wrath of God, which is poured out without mixture into the cup of his **indignation**; and he shall be tormented with fire and brimstone in the presence of the holy angels, and in the presence of the Lamb: **(11)** And the smoke of their torment ascendeth up for ever and ever: and they have no rest day nor night, who worship the beast and his image, and whosoever receiveth the mark of his name. **(12)** Here is the patience of the saints: here are they that keep the **commandments** of God, and the faith of Jesus. **(13)** And I heard a voice from Heaven saying unto me, Write, Blessed are the dead which die in the Lord from henceforth: Yea, saith the Spirit, that they may rest from their labours; and their works do follow them.

---

everlasting (GRK: αἰώνιον/ahee-o'-nee-on): Eternal; unending character; God's life at work in the believer; operating outside time, inside of time; beyond time.
gospel (GRK: εὐαγγέλιον/ yoo-ang-ghel'-ee-on): Glad tidings; good news (of the coming of the Messiah)
Babylon (GRK: Βαβυλών/ bab-oo-lone'): Gate of the gods; ancient city on the Euphrates; place of exile; wicked- godless city in ancient Mesopotamia.
fornication (GRK: πορνείας/ por-ni'-ahs) All immorality; fornication; whoredom; idolatry; (root-pornography); to sell off; sexual impurity; promiscuity.
indignation (GRK: θυμοῦ/ thuy-mou) Anger outburst; passion; wrath; God's holy wrath against sin.
commandments (GRK: ἐντολὰς/ en-tol-ais) an injunction, order or command; ordinance; law; consummation; end result of a command; highlights the nature of a specific order or charge.

Reflections on Revelation

ONE LAST CALL FROM GOD

In these verses we see God's angels proclaiming His message again to the Earth, just as they did in chapters eight and eleven. In those previous chapters, the angels flew "in the midst" of Heaven but the language here says that this angel is flying high above all things, like being at the very top of the universe. In these passages John uses the term "everlasting gospel" which is the only place in the Bible where this term is used. This good news of glad tidings (Lk. 2) has always been and will always be, and there is no way of avoiding the decision you must make about what you will believe. Since God's redemption cannot be earned by works, only received by faith (Eph. 2:8-9), then faith in this everlasting gospel is the choice that is set before all. The third angel completes this message and confirms the theme that there are no grey areas in choosing God over the dragon or the two beasts. If you take their mark it is unforgiveable, and the Greek here seems to point towards free ownership of the mark, not a forced decision. These messages to a sinful Earth almost seem like a first appearance in a court of law, where the charges are read, the penalty for those charges is announced, and then the incarcerated person waits for judgement. After this we see the loyalty and faith of the Saints of God being acknowledged. This faith is now an object lesson to those of Earth who have rebelled against God. They are praised by God for their patience and steadfast service in the midst of the evil of the world. (Gen 19; Gen 6; 2 Tim. 3:1-5). Christ can be found here in His plan to reward and acknowledge faith and patience in his children. The redemption and grace that even now are available to all is going to be worth every trial and tribulation.

---

1. Why is decision-based faith so unpopular in our world today, and how can any escape this decision?
2. What does the term "everlasting Gospel" mean?
3. What insights did you gain from the word studies from this session?
4. Share your thoughts and questions from this week's study.

Assigned for next session: (1) Read Revelation chapter fourteen daily; (2) Journal and record thoughts and questions; (3) Complete session #35 for next class; (reading for next session**:** Isaiah 5-34-63; Joel 3; Mat.3-10-13-24; Luke 17-21; Heb. 13; John 5-15; Acts 10; 2 Timothy 3-4).

NOTES

Notes

Session 35

FINDING CHRIST IN THE BOOK OF REVELATION

Revelation 14:14-20 (KJV)

REAPING THE EARTH'S HARVEST

(14) And I looked, and behold a white cloud, and upon the cloud one sat like unto the Son of man, having on his head a golden crown, and in his hand a sharp sickle. **(15)** And another angel came out of the temple, crying with a loud voice to him that sat on the cloud, Thrust in thy sickle, and **reap**: for the time is come for thee to reap; for the ***harvest*** of the Earth is ripe. **(16)** And he that sat on the cloud thrust in his sickle on the Earth; and the Earth was reaped. **(17)** And another angel came out of the temple which is in Heaven, he also having a sharp sickle. **(18)** And another angel came out from the altar, which had power over fire; and cried with a loud cry to him that had the sharp sickle, saying, Thrust in thy sharp sickle, and gather the clusters of the vine of the Earth; for her grapes are fully ripe. **(19)** And the angel thrust in his sickle into the Earth, and gathered the vine of the Earth, and cast it into the great winepress of the wrath of God. **(20)** And the winepress was trodden without the city, and blood came out of the winepress, even unto the horse bridles, by the space of a thousand and six hundred furlongs.

---

reap (GRK: θέρισον/ ther-i-son): Gather, harvest; to remove the wicked inhabitants of the Earth and deliver them up to destruction.
harvest (GRK: θερισμός/ ther-is-mos'): The act of reaping; the gathering of men into God; final judgment; righteous are saved, wicked delivered to destruction.

Reflections on Revelation

THE SECOND COMING OF CHRIST

Building a general understanding of what these verses tell us about the end of the tribulation and the start of the final war against evil is relatively easy if you know what to look for. The unmistakable theme of these verses is to see Christ as the final judge who is bringing an end to grace and the Great Commission, as we see the redemptive power of the Spirit of God leaving the Earth and being replaced with the power of judgement. This would signify that all who can be saved have been saved, and Israel has been restored. Some feel this is a picture of the culmination of the entire history of the church from the resurrection until the second coming. However, these verses tell a story of judgement and not of gathering. There are three main harvests spoken of in the Bible: barley, wheat, and the fruit of the vine or grapes. They all represent the gathering of souls, but barley is left out of consideration here because these events center on the harvest of grapes and wheat, which were fall events. The barley was the first harvest coming at the Passover celebration or in the spring of the year. This is significant as it is a sign of the first harvest, new life, and of the church being raptured. Barley made the bread Jesus used to feed the 5000, and is an example of God's provision to mankind, which we can see has now ended. The winepress here is unique in scripture as its purpose is to express God's wrath, thus the term the grapes of wrath. This is why many believe these events represent the second coming of Christ leading up to the great war against evil. In the Bible, the wheat harvest always represented salvation and grapes were always an example of the justification and redemption processes (John 15). Now the time for salvation on Earth has finished, and if the harvest is over then so is the tribulation. Jesus then turns the cleanup of the harvest over to His warring angels, which involves pruning, cutting, clearing, and burning. In the Bible, pruning is a metaphor for God's correction, but this pruning is about judgement. The chaff is always an example of those who refused salvation and are cut off from God to be burned, so this is about the cutting off of the dead branches and useless fruit to be cast away. This winepress, built for judgement, is also cast out after use, representing the end of all harvests. The last press brought blood, a symbol of a great and final battle, and being outside the city gates is symbolic of the place where all the unwanted trash and animal sacrifices were taken to be burned. This is also where Jesus was taken to be crucified. It's a place to exact punishment, and now Jesus is taking all who are left on Earth there. The blood, covering 200 miles, is estimated to take nearly eight million deaths. Finding Christ in these verses is to see the end of the rebellion of sin.

---

1. What did you learn from these verses?
2. What is happening here and what does it mean?
3. Is this a picture of the end of grace and the Great Commission?
4. What insights did you gain from the word studies in this session?
5. Share your thoughts and questions from this week's study.

Assigned for next session: (1) Read Revelation chapter fifteen daily; (2) Journal and record thoughts and questions; (3) Complete session #36 for next class.

NOTES

Notes

Session 36

THE BOOK OF REVELATION

Revelation 15:1-8 (KJV)

PRELUDE TO THE BOWL JUDGMENTS

(1) And I saw another sign in Heaven, great and marvelous, seven angels having the seven last **plagues**; for in them is filled up the wrath of God. **(2)** And I saw as it were a sea of glass mingled with fire: and them that had gotten the victory over the beast, and over his image, and over his mark, and over the number of his name, stand on the sea of glass, having the harps of God. **(3)** And they sing the song of Moses the servant of God, and the song of the Lamb, saying, Great and marvelous are thy works, Lord God Almighty; **just** and true are thy ways, thou King of saints. (4) Who shall not fear thee, O Lord, and glorify thy name? for thou only art holy: for all nations shall come and worship before thee; for thy judgments are made manifest. **(5)** And after that I looked, and, behold, the temple of the **tabernacle** of the testimony in Heaven was opened: **(6)** And the seven angels came out of the temple, having the seven plagues, clothed in pure and white linen, and having their breasts girded with golden girdles. **(7)** And one of the four beasts gave unto the seven angels seven golden vials full of the wrath of God, who liveth for ever and ever. **(8)** And the temple was filled with smoke from the glory of God, and from his power; and no man was able to enter into the temple, till the seven plagues of the seven angels were **fulfilled**.

---

plagues (GRK: πληγὰς/ Play-gas): A blow or wound; a beating; affliction; death-stroke; public calamity.
fulfilled (GRK: ἐτελέσθη/ et-el-es-thay): Completion; an ending; to accomplish; consummation; reaching the end; to perform as commanded.
just (Lit: Righteous) (GRK: δίκαιαι/ dik'-ah-ay): Correct righteousness; innocence; right in the eyes of God; the elect of God; judicial approval; conformity to God's standard; upright.
tabernacle (GRK: σκηνῆς/ Skay-nais): A tent or hut; The tent of David; the Holy place; the Holy of holies; a mobile dwelling place where God chooses to live.

Reflections on Revelation

GOD'S DWELLING IS WITH HIS CREATION

In these verses we see a great image of the God who has chosen to be with His creation. He is not a cold or heartless God who enjoys destruction and judgement, but He has been forced to act against sin for the sake of His Kingdom. The sea like glass and fire seems to point to God's holy righteousness and purity that brings judgement. His judgements are not only penalties for sin but are intended to establish the final dominance over the dragon and the beasts. God is now allowing His children to see, as the final step to their salvation, His completed victory over sin, for it is His will that they witness it all. The songs of Moses and of the Lamb bring together God's perfect law from the Old Testament and the law of grace and life in Christ from the New Testament (Luke 22:19-20; Hebrews 10:4; Hebrews 8:8-12). All those who have been chosen by God, and who have accepted that choosing, have received the fullness of God. It is righteousness, sanctification, and justification all brought together in a completed work, and God's love has produced gratitude and respect from those who were once sinful but who now are completely innocent of sin. We can imagine that, as they watch the bowls of judgement poured out on the Earth, many will think "that could have been me." The Tabernacle, clearly in Heaven with God at the throne, is a symbol of God's mobile dwelling place that went from a tent, to the temple, to the indwelling of the Holy Spirit within God's children. They have become the living dwelling place of God and this is a great vision of God's desire for intimacy with His children. The seven plagues brought from the seven angels represent the byproduct of sin that is now being judged (Liv. 26). With this judgement we see God's power so strong that even the redeemed cannot stand within it (Ex. 40:34-35), this is His victory in this holy war against a fallen world (Acts 7:48-50; Acts 17:24; 1 Kings 8:27; 2 Chron. 2:6; Isaiah 66:1). There is evidence in the Bible that a stationary temple was never God's plan, but He allowed it for the desire of Israel. Now His better plan is in place, to dwell with His children and be their personal and corporate God. With no more restrictions from a fallen world, the temple and tabernacle are one, and we can and will find Jesus there, dwelling with and in His creation!

---

1. Why are these last plagues necessary?
2. Can God's children experience this relationship now?
3. What insights did you gain from the word studies in this session?
4. Share your thoughts and questions from this week's study.

Assigned for next session: (1) Read Revelation chapter sixteen daily; (2) Journal and record thoughts and questions; (3) Complete session #37 for next class.

Notes

Notes

Session 37

THE BOOK OF REVELATION

Revelation 16:1-21 (KJV)

THE SEVEN JUDGEMENTS (BOWLS)

(1) And I heard a great voice out of the temple saying to the seven angels, Go your ways, and pour out the **vials** of the wrath of God upon the Earth. **(2)** And the first went, and poured out his vial upon the Earth; and there fell a noisome and grievous **sore** upon the men which had the mark of the beast, and upon them which worshipped his image. **(3)** And the second angel poured out his vial upon the sea; and it became as the blood of a **dead man**: and every living soul died in the sea. **(4)** And the third angel poured out his vial upon the rivers and fountains of waters; and they became blood. **(5)** And I heard the angel of the waters say, Thou art righteous, O Lord, which art, and wast, and shalt be, because thou hast judged thus. (6) For they have shed the blood of saints and prophets, and thou hast given them blood to drink; for they are worthy. **(7)** And I heard another out of the altar say, Even so, Lord God Almighty, true and righteous are thy judgments. **(8)** And the fourth angel poured out his vial upon the sun; and power was given unto him to scorch men with fire. **(9)** And men were scorched with great heat, and blasphemed the name of God, which hath power over these plagues: and they repented not to give him glory. **(10)** And the fifth angel poured out his vial upon the seat of the beast; and his kingdom was full of darkness; and they gnawed their tongues for pain, **(11)** And blasphemed the God of Heaven because of their pains and their sores, and repented not of their deeds. **(12)** And the sixth angel poured out his vial upon the great river Euphrates; and the water thereof was dried up, that the way of the kings of the east might be prepared. **(13)** And I saw three unclean spirits like frogs come out of the mouth of the dragon, and out of the mouth of the beast, and out of the mouth of the false prophet. **(14)** For they are the spirits of devils, working miracles, which go forth unto the kings of the Earth and of the whole world, to gather them to the battle of that great day of God Almighty. **(15)** Behold, I come as a thief. Blessed is he that watcheth, and keepeth his garments, lest he walk naked, and they see his shame. **(16)** And he gathered them together into a place called in the Hebrew tongue Armageddon. **(17)** And the seventh angel poured out his vial into the air; and there came a great voice out of the temple of Heaven, from the throne, saying, It is done. **(18)** And there were voices, and thunders, and lightnings; and there was a great Earthquake, such as was not since men were upon the Earth, so mighty an Earthquake, and so great. **(19)** And the great city was divided into three parts, and the cities of the nations fell: and great Babylon came in remembrance before God, to give unto her the cup of the wine of the fierceness of his wrath. **(20)** And every island fled away, and the mountains were not found. **(21)** And there fell upon men a great hail out of Heaven, every stone about the weight of a talent: and men blasphemed God because of the plague of the hail; for the plague thereof was exceeding great.

---

vials (GRK: φιάλας/phai-las): Shallow bowl; flat cup.
sore (GRK: νεκροῦ / neck-rou): Festering ulcer.
dead man (GRK: νεκροῦ / neck-rou): Lifeless; subject to mortality; lacking life; unable to perform functions; ineffective; powerless; inoperative to the things of God.

Reflections on Revelation

THE VIALS OF FINAL JUDGEMENT

Here again we see sores, seas of blood, rivers of blood, scorched men, Earth with heat and drought, darkness and pain, and a great earthquake. Either this is a deeper and more descriptive account of the same judgements that occurred earlier in Revelation and like in Exodus, or God has issued new judgements that are very similar to those described before (Rev 8-11; Ex. 7-12). In Matthew 24 Jesus called this the time of "great distress," where there will be no reprieve from suffering. What is clear is that the last three chapters of Revelation describe God's plan to bring judgement and to put an end to the sin and rebellion perpetrated on the Earth by the dragon and his beasts. We can find Christ here in His commitment to never change in His love for his Saints and in His promises to us for peace and eternal life and joy.

---

1. Are these the same judgements as before?
2. Why are God's judgements justified?
3. What is prevenient grace, will it end?
4. Does the Great Commission end here? (I Tim. 2:1-4)
5. What insights did you gain from the word studies from this session?
6. Share your thoughts and questions from this week's study.

Assigned for next session: (1) Read Revelation chapter seventeen daily; (2) Journal and record thoughts and questions; (3) Complete session #38 for next class.

Notes

NOTES

Session 38 - A

THE BOOK OF REVELATION

Revelation 17:1-8 (KJV)

THE SCARLET WOMAN AND THE SCARLET BEAST

(1) And there came one of the seven angels which had the seven vials, and talked with me, saying unto me, Come hither; I will shew unto thee the judgment of the **great whore** that sitteth upon many waters: **(2)** With whom the kings of the Earth have committed fornication, and the inhabitants of the Earth have been made drunk with the wine of her fornication. **(3)** So he carried me away in the spirit into the wilderness: and I saw a woman sit upon a scarlet coloured beast, full of names of blasphemy, having seven heads and ten horns. **(4)** And the woman was arrayed in purple and scarlet colour, and decked with gold and precious stones and pearls, having a golden cup in her hand full of abominations and filthiness of her fornication: **(5)** And upon her forehead was a name written, **Mystery**, Babylon The Great, The Mother Of Harlots And Abominations Of The Earth. **(6)** And I saw the woman drunken with the blood of the saints, and with the blood of the martyrs of Jesus: and when I saw her, I wondered with great admiration. **(7)** And the angel said unto me, Wherefore didst thou marvel? I will tell thee the mystery of the woman, and of the beast that carrieth her, which hath the seven heads and ten horns. **(8)** The beast that thou sawest was, and is not; and shall ascend out of the bottomless pit, and go into **perdition**: and they that dwell on the Earth shall wonder, whose names were not written in the book of life from the foundation of the world, when they behold the beast that was, and is not, and yet is.

great whore (GRK: πόρνης-τῆς-μεγάλης / porn-ais tais mega-less): Harlot; prostitute; idolatrous community; Babylon; Rome, the chief seat of idolatry. (root word for pornography)
mystery (GRK: μυστήριον/ mus-tay-rion): A hidden secret; secret religious rites; A hidden purpose or counsel; the secret will of men; lawlessness beyond God's will.
perdition (GRK: ἀπώλειαν/ apo-lai-an): Destruction; completely severed from what should have been; cut off entirely from your rights; loss of well-being; voiding a covenant.

Reflections on Revelation

THE SEED OF SIN

Many see these verses as a description and explanation of the seven bowl judgements we studied previously, and due to the presence of one of the seven angels this is a reasonable view. As John is stricken with awe at what he is currently seeing, one of the seven angels must comfort him and describe to him in more detail exactly what he is witnessing. The term harlot here is seen as Babylon the Great, or the evil influences that give sin and false religions their power in the hearts of man. There are extensive readings on the influences of Babylon and the great prostitute in Isaiah and Jeremiah (Isa. 13, 14, 47; and Jer. 50, 51). This whore is sinful mentality and corruption in the soul of humankind; she is the mother of all spiritual deception and is a metaphor for the combination of world powers and false religions that have deceived mankind since the fall and original sin (Genesis 3-4). This unlawful bonding with sin has created a mentality that fueled the world's hatred of God throughout history, because of God's stand against immorality and idol worship. This alliance between Satan and man and with everything that is anti-God is carnal by nature and is compared to being with a prostitute who gets drunk from drinking the blood of the weak and innocent. In other words, the world gets excited by destroying that which belongs to God. This vision leaves John the Apostle in amazement at the power sin has had over humankind and of the destruction Satan has brought to God's creation. God's Word warned of this carnal nature (2 Tim 3:1-5), and this spirit of Antichrist is alive in the world today. It is universalism, the new-age movement; existentialism, atheism, Gnosticism, humanism, paganism, and even faiths that claim to be Christian- based but that contradict God's Word and promote and justify sin. Many have tried to identify the harlot as a specific religion or nation, and this could be so, but it is more responsible to identify this in terms of the overall destructive power that false religion has displayed over the history of the world. We can find Christ in the knowledge that His deliverance from this deception is promised as we seek the Holy Spirit's guidance on a daily basis.

1. Why is John so stricken in this vision?
2. Discuss what the concept of the great harlot represents.
3. (Groups can either continue to 38-B or save that for the next session).

Notes

NOTES

Session 38 - B

THE BOOK OF REVELATION

Revelation 17:9-18 (KJV)

(9) And here is the mind which hath wisdom. The seven heads are seven mountains, on which the woman sitteth. **(10)** And there are seven kings: five are fallen, and one is, and the other is not yet come; and when he cometh, he must continue a short space. **(11)** And the beast that was, and is not, even he is the eighth, and is of the seven, and goeth into **perdition**. **(12)** And the ten horns which thou sawest are ten kings, which have received no kingdom as yet; but receive power as kings one hour with the beast. **(13)** These have one mind, and shall give their power and strength unto the beast. **(14)** These shall make war with the Lamb, and the Lamb shall overcome them: for he is Lord of lords, and King of kings: and they that are with him are called, and **chosen**, and faithful. **(15)** And he saith unto me, The waters which thou sawest, where the whore sitteth, are peoples, and multitudes, and nations, and tongues. **(16)** And the ten horns which thou sawest upon the beast, these shall hate the whore, and shall make her desolate and naked, and shall eat her flesh, and burn her with fire. **(17)** For God hath put in their hearts to fulfil his will, and to agree, and give their kingdom unto the beast, until the words of God shall be fulfilled. **(18)** And the woman which thou sawest is that great city, which reigneth over the kings of the Earth.

---

chosen (GRK: ἐκλεκτοὶ/ e-kleck-toi): Favorite; the elect of God; Hebrew race; the Messiah; chosen to obtain salvation through Christ; called to be the elect of God.

Reflections on Revelation

THE SEED OF SIN, CONTINUED . . .

Again, in these verses, God is challenging us to use wisdom in trying to understand these mysteries. In a sense, He is saying that the reader should not get drawn into fantastic and judgmental beliefs about which religions will lead the way into these deceptions or to what actual world powers will be represented. As we discussed in the introduction to this study, we should pray and seek God's Spirit for guidance. Many feel that these seven mountains are the seven hills of Rome. However, it is a better interpretation to see these mountain tops as high places of power or kingships that have existed throughout history and have been opposed to God's will. They have been led by evil and sin and are in alliance with the spirit of Antichrist even thousands of years before the beasts of Satan will actually walk the Earth. Of these seven powers, we can hypothesize that the five that had already passed at the time of John's vision would include those that opposed Israel through their history. They are Egypt, Assyria, Babylon, Persia, and Greece. The other powers seem to be future entities, and all are welcome to try to guess what their identities are. The purpose for these world powers has always been the same: they are to join Satan to war against Jesus, the Lamb of God. They have tried to destroy Israel, the seed of Abraham and of King David, in order to eliminate God's power to fulfill prophesy in bringing the Messiah. Regardless of who or what they are, we must recognize that their roll in opposing God is more important than their actual identities. The beast and the spirit of Antichrist end up hating the harlot, which could be a picture of how those world powers and religions will resent Satan for demanding they give him their power and allegiance, for he will not share glory and power with any others. In this interpretation we can see how the world will finally awake to the realization that Satan is not for them, but is opposed to all. But by this time, they will have fallen too far and it will be too late to oppose the evil that they have allowed to take their power. Satan will use physical, emotional, and mental attacks to destroy all of those who brought him into power, as he is the ultimate betrayer and liar, and God wants the entire world to see him for what he is and to realize their folly. Finding Christ here is found in our understanding that, by faith, we will be immune to Satan's power to deceive, and by staying in God's Spirit daily we can see the truth even when a lost world cannot.

---

1. Why do the beast and Babylon betray the harlot?
2. What does the term perdition mean to you?
3. Is Babylon going to also be an actual city?
4. What insights did you gain from the word studies from this session?
5. Share your thoughts and questions from this week's study.

Assigned for next session: (1) Read Revelation chapter eighteen daily; (2) Journal and record thoughts and questions; (3) Complete session #39 for next class.

NOTES

NOTES

Session 39

THE BOOK OF REVELATION

Revelation 18:1-8 (KJV)

THE FALL OF BABYLON

(1) And after these things I saw another angel come down from Heaven, having great power; and the Earth was **lightened** with his glory. **(2)** And he cried mightily with a strong voice, saying, Babylon the great is fallen, is fallen, and is become the habitation of devils, and the hold of every foul spirit, and **a cage** of every unclean and hateful bird. **(3)** For all nations have drunk of the wine of the wrath of her fornication, and the kings of the Earth have committed fornication with her, and the merchants of the Earth are waxed rich through the abundance of her delicacies. **(4)** And I heard another voice from Heaven, saying, Come out of her, my people, that ye be not partakers of her sins, and that ye receive not of her plagues. **(5)** For her sins have reached unto Heaven, and God hath remembered her **iniquities**. **(6)** Reward her even as she rewarded you, and double unto her double according to her works: in the cup which she hath filled fill to her double. **(7)** How much she hath glorified herself, and lived deliciously, so much torment and sorrow give her: for she saith in her heart, I sit a queen, and am no widow, and shall see no sorrow. **(8)** Therefore shall her plagues come in one day, death, and mourning, and famine; and she shall be utterly burned with fire: for strong is the Lord God who **judgeth** her.

---

lightened (GRK: ἐφωτίσθη / Ep-pho-tis-thay): Illuminated, shine, give light; bring to light-wisdom; make evident; reveal; God's life; expose and overcome darkness; push out ignorance, prejudice, caused by sin.
a cage (GRK: φυλακὴ/ phy-lock-ay): A Prison; To guard or watch; imprisonment at the night watch of darkness.
iniquities (GRK: ἀδικήματα / adi-que-mata): Sin; Wrongful injury; legal wrong; crime against God; evidence to charge; unrighteousness; violation of God's justice; judgments with divine retribution.
judges (GRK: krínō / kri-no): Separate-distinguish for judgement; make a decision; determine right or wrong, innocence or guilt; official legal standard; to approve what is correct; reject what is inferior; bringing to trial.

Reflections on Revelation

GOD'S JUDGEMENT EXPLAINED

John now sees another angel, one so filled with God's glory that the light drives Babylon straight into the pit of Hell. All darkness and sin everywhere have been eradicated. The authority of this angel has illuminated the darkest day in Earth's history and filled it with God's light. With this comes the announcement that Babylon is fallen, literally meaning "dropped to Hell" and the place which was the throne room of Satan is now a prison used to incarcerate all evil entities condemned by God. The idol that the world followed is now seen in its true light as a jail cell and a place of bondage. To the church, this message of God's light coming to drive out evil would have been welcomed and rejoiced over. The merchants or travelers, literally translated as lost wanderers, have been engaged in this rebellion and sin and have become rich in their minds, but are very lost and poor spiritually (Revelation 3:17). They will go into captivity and domination forever, and just as in the time when Moses discovered the Children of Israel in sin, and as God commanded his people to come out from the congregation of sinners just before the ground opened and swallowed them (Num. 16), we see that the lost will see the Earth open again and swallow up those in rebellion. This message to the church, that rebellion against God will bring a greater price than any punishment the world can inflict, is a warning of love. It is also encouragement that God's children need to be on fire for their faith and should stay on the path of righteousness. Lay aside all lukewarm religion and be children of God, for His wrath and judgement will be a crushing blow when Babylon falls. Some believe that the great angel in these passages could be Christ or the Holy Spirit, as the holiness of God shines through this being. What is sure is that the last battle, or Armageddon, is a victory, though it will be bloody and all-consuming. God's light will shine on Earth and drive out darkness (John 1:5; John 3:19; 1 John 2:11; John 8:12; John 1:4-5). Our message today is that Jesus wants to give us His light, and we can find Christ in this study by remembering to shine.

---

1. Who is this Angel of Light?
2. Is this the great war after the second coming?
3. Is the tribulation over?
4. What is the significance of the fall of Babylon?
5. To the churches of that day, what would this message of Babylon's fall mean?
6. What insights did you gain from the word studies from this session?
7. Share your thoughts and questions from this week's study.

Assigned for next session: (1) Read Revelation chapter eighteen daily; (2) Journal and record thoughts and questions; (3) Complete session #40 for next class.

NOTES

NOTES

Session 40

THE BOOK OF REVELATION

Revelation 18:9-24 (KJV)

THE WORLD MOURNS BABYLON'S FALL

(9) And the kings of the Earth, who have committed fornication and lived deliciously with her, shall **bewail** her, and **lament** for her, when they shall see the smoke of her burning, **(10)** Standing afar off for the fear of her torment, saying, Alas, alas that great city Babylon, that mighty city! for in one hour is thy judgment come. **(11)** And the merchants of the Earth shall weep and mourn over her; for no man buyeth their merchandise any more: **(12)** The merchandise of gold, and silver, and precious stones, and of pearls, and fine linen, and purple, and silk, and scarlet, and all thyine wood, and all manner vessels of ivory, and all manner vessels of most precious wood, and of brass, and iron, and marble, **(13)** And cinnamon, and odours, and ointments, and frankincense, and wine, and oil, and fine flour, and wheat, and beasts, and sheep, and horses, and chariots, and slaves, and souls of men. **(14)** And the fruits that thy soul lusted after are departed from thee, and all things which were dainty and goodly are departed from thee, and thou shalt find them no more at all. **(15)** The merchants of these things, which were made rich by her, shall stand afar off for the fear of her torment, weeping and wailing, **(16)** And saying, Alas, alas that great city, that was clothed in fine linen, and purple, and scarlet, and decked with gold, and precious stones, and pearls! **(17)** For in one hour so great riches is come to nought. And every shipmaster, and all the company in ships, and sailors, and as many as trade by sea, stood afar off, **(18)** And cried when they saw the smoke of her burning, saying, What city is like unto this great city! **(19)** And they cast dust on their heads, and cried, weeping and wailing, saying, Alas, alas that great city, wherein were made rich all that had ships in the sea by reason of her costliness! for in one hour is she made desolate. **(20)** Rejoice over her, thou Heaven, and ye holy apostles and prophets; for God hath avenged you on her. **(21)** And a mighty angel took up a stone like a great millstone, and cast it into the sea, saying, Thus with violence shall that great city Babylon be thrown down, and shall be found no more at all. **(22)** And the voice of harpers, and musicians, and of pipers, and trumpeters, shall be heard no more at all in thee; and no craftsman, of whatsoever craft he be, shall be found any more in thee; and the sound of a millstone shall be heard no more at all in thee; **(23)** And the light of a candle shall shine no more at all in thee; and the voice of the bridegroom and of the bride shall be heard no more at all in thee: for thy merchants were the great men of the Earth; for by thy sorceries were all nations deceived. **(24)** And in her was found the blood of prophets, and of saints, and of all that were slain upon the Earth.

---

bewail (GRK: κλαύσουσιν/ Klaus-ou-sin): Weep; mourn; lament; audible grief; to bewail.
Lament (GRK: Κόψονται / kops-on-tai): To cut off; to mourn; to smite; to be incised and severed; a cutting sense of personal, tragic loss to the heart.

Reflections on Revelation

THE DESTRUCTION OF HUMANISM

It seems that this is the aftermath of Armageddon, and the kings of the Earth are stricken with awe over the swift justice that has befallen all who followed Satan. The online dictionary defines humanism as, "an outlook or system of thought attaching prime importance to human rather than divine or supernatural matters," and we see how this mentality will suddenly and forcefully come to an end. From here we see the bitterness and resentment that fuels the world's desire to oppose God come forth again, and their motivation will be for revenge from a narcissistic sense of injustice. The world will no longer be deceived about their Creator but will still openly oppose righteousness! The world's system will grieve and mourn this loss, as their greatest love will be gone forever. Even after all things of Earth, including physical life, have been exposed as carnal, it will remain the god that controls the hearts of many. Babylon, the great harlot, the kings of the Earth, the beasts (of which one is the Antichrist), and the dragon are now defeated, forever. And though there is evidence that the lost will continue in sin, the greatest gift to God's Children is not streets or crowns of gold, or crystal seas, but it will be the destruction of their personal sin nature that has tormented them throughout their lives. That's where we find Christ in these verses (John 8).

---

1. What is the world mourning for?
2. What insights did you gain from the word studies from this session?
3. Share your thoughts and questions from this week's study.

Assigned for next session: (1) Read Revelation chapter nineteen daily; (2) Journal and record thoughts and questions; (3) Complete session #41 for next class.

NOTES

Notes

SESSION 41

THE BOOK OF REVELATION

REVELATION 19:1-10 (KJV)

HEAVEN EXULTS OVER BABYLON

(1) And after these things I heard a great voice of much people in Heaven, saying, **Alleluia**; Salvation, and glory, and honour, and power, unto the Lord our God: **(2)** For true and **righteous** are his judgments: for he hath judged the great whore, which did **corrupt** the Earth with her fornication, and hath avenged the blood of his servants at her hand. **(3)** And again they said, Alleluia And her smoke rose up for ever and ever. **(4)** And the four and twenty elders and the four beasts fell down and worshipped God that sat on the throne, saying, Amen; Alleluia. **(5)** And a voice came out of the throne, saying, Praise our God, all ye his servants, and ye that fear him, both small and great. **(6)** And I heard as it were the voice of a great multitude, and as the voice of many waters, and as the voice of mighty **thunderings**, saying, Alleluia: for the Lord God **omnipotent** reigneth. **(7)** Let us be glad and rejoice, and give honour to him: for the marriage of the Lamb is come, and his wife hath made herself ready. **(8)** And to her was granted that she should be arrayed in fine linen, clean and white: for the fine linen is the righteousness of saints. **(9)** And he saith unto me, Write, Blessed are they which are called unto the marriage supper of the Lamb. And he saith unto me, These are the true sayings of God. **(10)** And I fell at his feet to worship him. And he said unto me, See thou do it not: I am thy fellowservant, and of thy brethren that have the testimony of Jesus: worship God: for the testimony of Jesus is the spirit of prophecy.

---

alleluia (GRK: Ἀλληλουϊά / all-ay-lu-jah): Hallelujah; adoring exclamation; Praise to God; praise Yahweh.
righteous (GRK: δίκαιαι / dik-ay-ai): Correct; innocent; justness of God; judicial approval of God; conformity to God's standard; upright.
corrupted (GRK: ἔφθειρεν / ep-thay-ren): To destroy or ruin; perish or waste away; deteriorate; moral deterioration; decomposition; becoming a lower form.
thunderings (GRK: βροντῶν / braun-ton): Peals of thunder; a roar with overwhelming power.
omnipotent (GRK: Παντοκράτωρ / pan-to-krat-or): The almighty ruler of all; the unrestricted power exercising absolute dominion; He who holds sway over all things; Jehovah or God of hosts; the omnipotent being or the God who has absolute and universal sovereign power.

REFLECTIONS ON REVELATION

THE MARRIAGE SUPPER OF THE LAMB

Sin's reign on Earth is over, and though there is evidence that rebellion will still exist during the thousand-year reign, we now see the church and the restored nation of Israel being clothed in white and coming to the marriage supper of the Lamb. This is the culmination of God's plan to reunite with His creation, and there is celebration for this victory (Mt. 22:2-10). The final day of the tribulation has ended, and God's children show their appreciation, love, and dedication to their God and savior while Babylon is still a burning dungeon for the rebellious who lost a futile war against God. In verse six we see the only place in scripture where the word omnipotent is used, this word translated as the Almighty Ruler of all, and the marriage of Christ to the church is a metaphor for God's children being united with their Almighty Ruler forever. After the great battle, the warriors and saints of God, both Gentile and Jews, will come to a great celebration and feast. This vision is so spectacular that John falls before the angel delivering this vision to him and worships, which the angel quickly forbids. In coming chapters, we will see the war that has been won in greater detail, but for now we find Christ in the assurance of victory and the church's ultimate and eternal destiny to be with Him.

---

1. Who will be invited to the Marriage Supper of the Lamb?
2. What is the Marriage supper of the Lamb going to be like?
3. Will this event be the first time in history that Messianic Jews and Christian Gentiles have come together to worship God?
4. What insights did you gain from the word studies from this session?
5. Share your thoughts and questions from this week's study.

Assigned for next session: (1) Read Revelation chapter nineteen daily; (2) Journal and record thoughts and questions; (3) Complete session #42 for next class.

NOTES

NOTES

Session 42

THE BOOK OF REVELATION

Revelation 19:11-21 (KJV)

MESSIAH ON A WHITE HORSE

(11) And I saw Heaven opened, and behold a white horse; and he that sat upon him was called Faithful and True, and in righteousness he doth judge and make war. **(12)** His eyes were as a flame of fire, and on his head were many **crowns**; and he had a name written, that no man knew, but he himself. **(13)** And he was clothed with a vesture dipped in blood: and his name is called The Word of God. **(14)** And the **armies** which were in Heaven followed him upon white horses, clothed in fine linen, white and clean. **(15)** And out of his mouth goeth a **sharp sword**, that with it he should smite the nations: and he shall rule them with a rod of iron: and he treadeth the winepress of the fierceness and wrath of Almighty God. **(16)** And he hath on his vesture and on his thigh a name written, King Of Kings, And Lord Of Lords. **(17)** And I saw an angel standing in the sun; and he cried with a loud voice, saying to all the fowls that fly in the midst of Heaven, Come and gather yourselves together unto the supper of the great God; **(18)** That ye may eat the flesh of kings, and the flesh of captains, and the flesh of mighty men, and the flesh of horses, and of them that sit on them, and the flesh of all men, both free and bond, both small and great. **(19)** And I saw the beast, and the kings of the Earth, and their armies, gathered together to make war against him that sat on the horse, and against his army. **(20)** And the beast was taken, and with him the false prophet that wrought miracles before him, with which he deceived them that had received the mark of the beast, and them that worshipped his image. These both were cast alive into a lake of fire burning with brimstone. **(21)** And the remnant were slain with the sword of him that sat upon the horse, which sword proceeded out of his mouth: and all the fowls were filled with their flesh.

---

crowns (GRK: διαδήματα / dia-day-mata): Royal diadem; a head-wreath; kingly ornament for the head.
armies (GRK: στρατεύματα / Strat-ou-mata) an expedition; an army; a company of soldiers; a detachment of troops.
sharp (GRK: ὀξεῖα/ oacks-ay-ya) sharp; swift or eager.
sword (GRK: ῥομφαία/ rhoam-phai-a) a sword or scimitar; for war; piercing grief; a long Thracian sword; a large, broad sword that both cuts and pierces; an imposing sword, synonymous with finality and dominance.

Reflections on Revelation

THE RIDER IN WHITE

John now specifically describes Christ going into battle as the general of the armies of God. This Lamb is not portrayed as meek or mild-mannered, but is shown as fierce and with garments stained, or literally moistened, with blood. We again see Jesus' Word as a sharp weapon intended to uphold God's purpose and used to protect God's Kingdom from the destruction of sin. The word sharp, in verse fifteen, means "swift, true, and eager," and whatever Jesus speaks into existence becomes real in an instant (Numbers 23:19). The last time we saw this description of Jesus was when he opened the scroll with the seven seals in Revelation six, seven, and eight. These verses use a form of writing called apologetics, which is a reasoned argument or writing used in justification of something. Jesus here is justified, and just as in chapter one, His eyes are flames of fire, or "bright, swirling, and glowing." This is a representation of the knowledge that Christ has above all; He knows all, and nothing is beyond His sight (Hebrews 4:11-13). Those who follow Christ know that the outcome of this war is already set and that in the aftermath Jesus will rule with a "rod of iron" (Rev. 19:15). The words literally mean "an iron scepter" and only a King gets to wield a scepter, which is a symbol of authority. Before this, people had a choice to follow God or not, but now Jesus, along with His ruling saints, will guide and correct all, throughout eternity. The final judgement after the thousand-year reign is yet to come, but we again are reminded that those who walked according to the lusts of their flesh will see that same flesh, literally, be devoured by wild birds and animals. After this, there will only be Christ and His bride, with God, forever. That is where we find our Savior, in the assurance of His faithfulness.

---

1. In this description of the final battle, what stands out to you as most important to recognize?
2. What's the gospel message in these verses?
3. What insights did you gain from the word studies from this session?
4. Share your thoughts and questions from this week's study.

Assigned for next session: (1) Read Revelation chapter twenty daily; (2) Journal and record thoughts and questions; (3) Complete session #43 for next class.

NOTES

NOTES

Session 43

THE BOOK OF REVELATION

Revelation 20:1-6 (KJV)

SATAN BOUND 1,000 YEARS

(1) And I saw an angel come down from Heaven, having the key of the bottomless pit and a great chain in his hand. **(2)** And he **laid hold** on the dragon, that old serpent, which is the Devil, and Satan, and bound him a thousand years, **(3)** And cast him into the bottomless pit, and **shut** him up, and set a **seal** upon him, that he should **deceive** the nations no more, till the thousand years should be fulfilled: and after that he must be loosed a little season. **(4)** And I saw thrones, and they sat upon them, and judgment was given unto them: and I saw the souls of them that were beheaded for the witness of Jesus, and for the word of God, and which had not worshipped the beast, neither his image, neither had received his mark upon their foreheads, or in their hands; and they lived and reigned with Christ a thousand years. **(5)** But the rest of the dead lived not again until the thousand years were finished. This is the first **resurrection.** **(6)** Blessed and holy is he that hath part in the first resurrection: on such the second death hath no power, but they shall be priests of God and of Christ, and shall reign with him a thousand years.

---

laid hold (GRK: ἐκράτησεν/ eckra-tais-ein): Seize with strength; to rule; to prevail over; put under control.
shut (GRK: κλείω/ kli'-o): To shut up.
sealed (GRK: ἐσφράγισεν/ es-phra-gi-sen): Seal with a signet ring or stamp; to have a legal signature.
deceive (GRK: πλανάω / plan-ah'-o): Cause to wander; lead astray; deceive; lead off-course; deviate from the correct path; roam into error; misled; wandering body.
resurrection (GRK: ἀνάστασις/ ana-stay-sis): Standing up resurrected; raised again; (Jn 6:39-44).

Reflections on Revelation

THE GREAT WAR REVIEWED

These verses that describe the start of the Millennial Kingdom show the victory celebration in Heaven and afterwards, when God binds up Satan and his minions and casts them into the pit of Hell for a thousand years. During this time Satan will no longer have the power to deceive men, a power he had held since the fall of man and the original sin (Genesis 1-2). This power to deceive is not restored until the end of the millennial reign, and then Satan's character will be exposed again, only for a moment, at the great white throne judgement (Rev. 20:11-14). It seems like this binding could be God's way of showing that sin is a personal choice, and if you sin now, during the thousand years, you cannot blame Satan for your rebellion. Then we see God's hierarchy in a picture of the thrones of Heaven. These are like those spoken of in Revelation four and will probably consist of the four and twenty elders, and other patriarchs from both the Old and New Testaments. During the millennial reign, the elders of the faith, with Christ and all the saints, will rule together by the power of God, in the unity that comes from the indwelling of the Holy Spirit. In verses four through six, many have argued that when Satan is bound, death will continue and those who were not redeemed and who did not die before the second advent of Christ will live in the thousand-year reign (Isaiah 65:17-25). At this point the condition of all of the other eternal souls from history is not known, but we know God's children will not be left in the grave (Heb. 9:27; Jn. 11:25-26; 1 Jn. 5:11; Jn. 3:16; I. Jn 5:20; Ps. 37:18; I Cor. 15:55; Jn. 6:27; Jn. 10:27-28; Jn. 4:14). Remember that those who are in Christ will never be left or forsaken (Gal. 3:26-28; Heb. 13:5), and that nowhere in the Bible does it mention a second death for God's redeemed. The best way to understand these deaths is that when a person becomes born again (John 3), they can still die a physical death on Earth. This is the first death. However, they will not suffer the second death, which is eternal separation from God in Hell. Only those who died physically and then were cast into Hell will experience this second death (Rev.2:11; Rev.20:6; Rev. 20:14; Rev. 21:8). So, we have three groups identified in the millennial reign: the dead in Christ who are raised first at the rapture; the saved who are raptured with them (I Thess. 4:16-17); and the lost who survived the tribulation to still be on Earth and alive when the millennial reign starts. It seems possible that all other souls who were dead and lost will not be raised until the great white throne judgement after the thousand-year reign.

---

1. Will death remain in the Millennial Kingdom?
2. When Satan is bound, will there be sin in the Millennial Kingdom?
3. What insights did you gain from the word studies in this session?
4. Share your thoughts and questions from this week's study.

Assigned for next session: (1) Read Revelation chapter twenty daily; (2) Journal and record thoughts and questions; (3) Complete session #44 for next class.

NOTES

Notes

Session 44

THE BOOK OF REVELATION

Revelation 20:7-15 (KJV)

SATANIC REBELLION CRUSHED

(7) And when the thousand years are expired, Satan shall be loosed out of his prison, **(8)** And shall go out to deceive the nations which are in the four quarters of the Earth, Gog, and Magog, to gather them together to battle: the number of whom is as the sand of the sea. **(9)** And they went up on the breadth of the Earth, and compassed the camp of the saints about, and the beloved city: and fire came down from God out of Heaven, and devoured them. **(10)** And the devil that deceived them was cast into the lake of fire and brimstone, where the beast and the false prophet are, and shall be tormented day and night for ever and ever.

(11) And I saw a great white throne, and him that sat on it, from whose face the Earth and the Heaven fled away; and there was found no place for them. **(12)** And I saw the **dead**, **small** and **great**, stand before God; and the books were opened: and another book was opened, which is the book of life: and the dead were judged out of those things which were written in the books, according to their works. **(13)** And the sea gave up the dead which were in it; and death and Hell delivered up the dead which were in them: and they were judged every man according to their works. **(14)** And death and Hell were cast into the lake of fire. This is the second death. **(15)** And whosoever was not found written in the book of life was cast into the lake of fire.

Dead (GRK: νεκρούς / nek-ros'): Lifeless; subject to mortality; a corpse; lacking life; ineffective; powerless; unresponsive; inoperative to the things of God.
Small (GRK: μικρούς / mik-ros'): The least; short; brief.
Great (GRK: μεγάλους / meg'-a-lous): Large; abundant; arrogant; completely fierce; high and mighty; huge; a long time.

Reflections on Revelation

THE GREAT WHITE THRONE JUDGEMENT

The release of Satan from the pit of Hell is only for the purpose of the final judgement. Once this happens his true character immediately comes out, as he again attempts to lead the Earth in rebellion against God. Gog, mentioned in verse eight, was one of the sons of Joel found in I Chronicles chapter five. Ezekiel goes to Gog, in the land of Magog, and prophesies against him. This was after Ezekiel raised the army of bones when his mission for God was to "unite" the houses of Israel under one king and one God (Ez. 37-38). Gog and his rebels surround God's camp in Jerusalem and are immediately consumed by Heaven's fire. The comparison to these verses is a simple concept. The final judgement will be to destroy all those opposed to the Kingdom of God. Now we not only see the physical bodies cast to Hell, but also the soul and spirits of those who carry rebellious thoughts and attitudes against God. This is the completed work of the Kingdom of God, to send out all corruption and false authorities based in human narcissistic deceptions. In the end, all the lost from Earth's history are raised and pass before the great white throne of God to be judged. This judgement is for the crime of blasphemy of the Holy Spirit (Luke 12:10; Matt. 12:32; Mark 3:29), which can be interpreted as the rejection of salvation while knowing the truth, and then standing before God's judgement without Christ's covering for sin. Having denied the work of the Holy Spirit, through salvation, and then to be judged without the covering of the blood of the Lamb is unforgivable. They have no covering, no great high priest, no shepherd, no king, and no savior. Now God's throne is no longer clouded in mist, but we see it clearly in God's light. God has no more secrets and no more whisperings, He is completely transparent and the unredeemed are judged in full site of His Glory. They pass right in front of that which they rejected, and as they face the Holy Trinity, they are uncovered, naked, and barren. The goats will be separated from the sheep and sent away (Matt. 25:31–46), but, before they go, all from Heaven, and Earth, and under the Earth, will bow before God and confess Jesus as Lord (Phil. 2:10-11). Those whose names are written in the Lamb's Book of Life are not here to be judged, but to be witnesses of God's justice (John 12:47-48). This is the end of the old and the beginning of the new (I Cor. 15:24-28). The book is opened and read, the great celebration has happened, and the thousand-year reign is finished.

---

1. What judgement will God's children face?
2. What feelings will God's Children have watching this judgement?
3. What insights did you gain from the word studies in this session?
4. Share your thoughts and questions from this week's study.

Assigned for next session: (1) Read Revelation chapter twenty-one daily; (2) Journal and record thoughts and questions; (3) Complete session #45 for next class.

NOTES

Notes

Session 45

THE BOOK OF REVELATION

Revelation 21:1-8 (KJV)

ALL THINGS MADE NEW

(1) And I saw a **new** Heaven and a new Earth: for the first Heaven and the first Earth were passed away; and there was no more sea. **(2)** And I John saw the holy city, new **Jerusalem**, coming down from God out of Heaven, prepared as a bride **adorned** for her husband. **(3)** And I heard a great voice out of Heaven saying, Behold, the tabernacle of God is with men, and he will dwell with them, and they shall be his people, and God himself shall be with them, and be their God. **(4)** And God shall wipe away all tears from their eyes; and there shall be no more death, neither sorrow, nor crying, neither shall there be any more pain: for the former things are passed away. **(5)** And he that sat upon the throne said, Behold, I make all things new. And he said unto me, Write: for these words are true and faithful. **(6)** And he said unto me, It is done. I am Alpha and Omega, the beginning and the end. I will give unto him that is athirst of the fountain of the water of life freely. **(7)** He that overcometh shall inherit all things; and I will be his God, and he shall be my son. **(8)** But the fearful, and unbelieving, and the abominable, and murderers, and whoremongers, and sorcerers, and idolaters, and all liars, shall have their part in the lake which burneth with fire and brimstone: which is the second death.

---

new (GRK: καινός/ kahee-nos'): Fresh; unused; novel; new in quality and development; not like before.
Jerusalem (GRK:Ἰερουσαλήμ/ hee-er-oo-sal-ame'): The capital of united Israel and Judah; The future Heavenly city and capital of God's peace; the Christian Church and the dwelling of peace.
adorned (GRK: ἡτοιμασμένην / he-toi-mas-men-en): Order or arrange; decorate or adorn; beautify; right arrangement or sequence; make compellingly attractive and inviting; awesomely gorgeous; (root of the Eng. term, "cosmetics,"); what adorns the face.

Reflections on Revelation

NEW HEAVEN, EARTH, AND JERUSALEM

John's vision now focuses on the Eternal Kingdom. He has seen Christ reign with a mighty hand while sin still had the ability to effect men. Now he sees the perfected vision of God, come down in a new Heaven and Earth. This is life without sin and a new Earth without corruption. Many feel that this is what the Garden of Eden might have been like before the fall of man, but we don't know for sure. The language here, and Christian tradition, suggests a new creation, literally new in every way (2 Cor. 5:17; Rom. 6:4; Jn. 1:10-13; Eph. 4:11-16). Before this, the Holy Spirit's power worked in regeneration while we were flesh and spirit, but now the flesh is changed, redeemed, new, and holy. In a sense, the first creation is no longer real, the new reality with nothing separating God from His creation is the original plan and all of the experiences of life will also be new. John's sermon or message of this vision, that started in chapter one of Revelation, now reaches its conclusion. The water of life is available to God's chosen and they will drink, and they will never go thirsty again. Jesus will share with us His blessings, including the new city of Jerusalem, which will no doubt have many places of wonder (John 14:1-4). Verse eight ends this segment with a reminder, a benediction or conclusion, that all saints need to remember; that the final destruction of the power of sin will come but until then we still have work to do. This message is to reconnect all of the church to the Great Commission Jesus gave at His ascension (Matt. 28:16-20). God wants a clean and spotless bride, the church, to be a companion to Jesus. We are to be His reward, and it boggles the mind to know God takes this much pleasure in His creation. The word commission means to be authorized to share, instruct, and to direct the lives of others. This task is to go into all the world, to make disciples of every nation, to teach those disciples to obey God's commands, and to baptize all as a symbol of new birth, an outward and visible sign of an inward and invisible faith. The promise and reward from this commission is eternal companionship, relationship, and intimacy with God. The "cowards" from verse eight are those who feared persecution and condemnation by men, and this reinforces the premise that it takes courage to follow God. Find Christ here, in your own power from God, to go forth in boldness to proclaim the good news of what awaits all of God's children.

---

1. Has this study changed your understanding of God?
2. What do verses three and four mean?
3. Why do the first Heaven and Earth pass away?
4. What insights did you gain from this session's word studies?
5. Share your thoughts and questions from this week's study.

Assigned for next session: (1) Read Revelation chapter 21 daily; (2) Journal and record your thoughts and questions; (3) Complete session #46 for next class.

NOTES

Notes

SESSION 46

THE BOOK OF REVELATION

REVELATION 21:9-27 (KJV)

THE NEW JERUSALEM, ITS GLORY

(9) And there came unto me one of the seven angels which had the seven vials full of the seven last plagues, and talked with me, saying, Come hither, I will shew thee the bride, the Lamb's wife. **(10)** And he carried me away in the spirit to a great and high mountain, and shewed me that great city, the holy Jerusalem, descending out of Heaven from God, **(11)** Having the glory of God: and her **light** was like unto a stone most precious, even like a jasper stone, clear as crystal; **(12)** And had a wall great and high, and had twelve gates, and at the gates twelve angels, and names written thereon, which are the names of the twelve tribes of the children of Israel: **(13)** On the east three gates; on the north three gates; on the south three gates; and on the west three gates. **(14)** And the wall of the city had twelve **foundations**, and in them the names of the twelve apostles of the Lamb. **(15)** And he that talked with me had a golden reed to measure the city, and the gates thereof, and the wall thereof. **(16)** And the city lieth foursquare, and the length is as large as the breadth: and he measured the city with the reed, twelve thousand furlongs. The length and the breadth and the height of it are equal. **(17)** And he measured the wall thereof, an hundred and forty and four cubits, according to the measure of a man, that is, of the angel. **(18)** And the building of the wall of it was of jasper: and the city was pure gold, like unto clear glass. **(19)** And the foundations of the wall of the city were garnished with all manner of precious stones. The first foundation was jasper; the second, sapphire; the third, a chalcedony; the fourth, an emerald; **(20)** The fifth, sardonyx; the sixth, sardius; the seventh, chrysolyte; the eighth, beryl; the ninth, a topaz; the tenth, a chrysoprasus; the eleventh, a jacinth; the twelfth, an amethyst. **(21)** And the twelve gates were twelve pearls: every several gate was of one pearl: and the street of the city was pure gold, as it were transparent glass. **(22)** And I saw no temple therein: for the Lord God Almighty and the Lamb are the temple of it. **(23)** And the city had no need of the sun, neither of the moon, to shine in it: for the glory of God did lighten it, and the Lamb is the light thereof. **(24)** And the nations of them which are saved shall walk in the light of it: and the kings of the Earth do bring their glory and honour into it. **(25)** And the gates of it shall not be shut at all by day: for there shall be no night there. **(26)** And they shall bring the glory and honour of the nations into it. **(27)** And there shall in no wise enter into it anything that defileth, neither whatsoever worketh abomination, or maketh a lie: but they which are written in the Lamb's book of life.

---

light (GRK: φωστήρ / foce-tare'): Luminary; illuminator; the sun or brilliant star; brightness.
Foundations (GRK:θεμέλιος/them-el'-ee-os): Stability; foundation stone; the beginning; the rudiment first principles of Christianity.

REFLECTIONS ON REVELATION

THE GREATEST CITY

John now goes to see the New Jerusalem, the Bride of Christ as she is called here. He is carried away again "in the spirit" as he was in chapters four and seventeen. John now writes a description of something so amazing it makes anything of Earth seem diminished or inconsequential. How can we imagine something greater than anything you can think of or imagine (Eph.3:20-21)? This New Jerusalem is described as being 1500 miles wide or taking up about the same space as the continental U.S. from the West Coast to the Appalachian Mountains. It is a gigantic and guarded city, but the gates will always be open. Who will attack God? This city has twelve gates named for the Twelve Tribes of Israel, and twelve foundations named for the Apostles who are symbolically now seen as a pathway or entrance to God in this holy place. In this city the sealed of God from Revelation seven, the Twelve Tribes of Israel, and all of the Gentiles who have been grafted into the vine, are part of the restored Body of Christ (Rom. 11). This city is similar in design to the original tabernacle of Moses, but it is of course much bigger (Ex. 24-26); and the twelve foundations, twelve gates, twelve apostles, and twelve tribes, all fit into God's plan to redeem mankind unto Himself, which is always where we can find Christ.

---

1. How does this vision impact your faith?
2. Is your name written in The Lambs Book of Life?
3. Why is New Jerusalem called "the Bride of Christ"?
4. What insights did you gain from this session's word studies?
5. Share your thoughts and questions from this week's study.

Assigned for next session: (1) Read Revelation chapter 22 daily; (2) Journal and record your thoughts and questions; (3) Complete session #47 for next class.

Notes

NOTES

Session 47

THE BOOK OF REVELATION

Revelations 22:1-11 (KJV)

THE RIVER OF LIFE

(1) And he shewed me a **pure** river of water of life, **clear** as **crystal,** proceeding out of the throne of God and of the Lamb. **(2)** In the midst of the street of it, and on either side of the river, was there the tree of life, which bare twelve manner of fruits, and yielded her fruit every month: and the leaves of the tree were for the healing of the nations. **(3)** And there shall be no more curse: but the throne of God and of the Lamb shall be in it; and his servants shall serve him: **(4)** And they shall see his face; and his name shall be in their foreheads. **(5)** And there shall be no night there; and they need no candle, neither light of the sun; for the Lord God giveth them light: and they shall reign for ever and ever. **(6)** And he said unto me, These sayings are faithful and true: and the Lord God of the holy prophets sent his angel to shew unto his servants the things which must shortly be done. **(7)** Behold, I come quickly: blessed is he that keepeth the sayings of the prophecy of this book. **(8)** And I John saw these things, and heard them. And when I had heard and seen, I fell down to worship before the feet of the angel which shewed me these things. **(9)** Then saith he unto me, See thou do it not: for I am thy fellowservant, and of thy brethren the prophets, and of them which keep the sayings of this book: worship God. **(10)** And he saith unto me, Seal not the sayings of the prophecy of this book: for the time is at hand. **(11)** He that is unjust, let him be unjust still: and he which is filthy, let him be filthy still: and he that is righteous, let him be righteous still: and he that is holy, let him be holy still.

---

pure: Lit- "clear as crystal".
clear (GRK: λαμπρός lam-pros') bright or shining; magnificent or splendid.
crystal (GRK: κρύσταλλον/kroos-tal-lon) crystal; a transparent precious stone; frost or ice; a rock crystal.

Reflections on Revelations

THE NEW CITY, A CLOSER LOOK

In these verses, John takes a closer look at New Jerusalem and specifically the river of life and the tree of life. This is a place of eternal living, and God's children will not thirst or hunger here (Rev. 21:6). The all-sufficient God is on His throne, and all the saved will have access to Him. In this account, at the time of all things being new, we see God's throne as Jesus' throne, they are one and the same. The tree of life is either a giant grove growing up in many places or it is many different trees, as the description in verse two suggests. Some have questioned why the nations continue to need healing, but just as the tree continues to provide nourishment for life, and the river water for thirst, so shall the leaves continue to provide healing for the unity of all. The idea is that God's covering and protection will never end, they are eternal. The curse, and all curses that came from the fall of man, are healed, or literally destroyed. This could mean that a continual protection from sin is now in place. All of God's chosen can now see Him face to face; it is the miracle of the bride and the Bridegroom. This message was so perplexing to John, in many ways, and he must have been wondering how this could be; but the angel confirms to him, in verse six, that it is all real. Then in verse seven, as in chapter one, John is assured of a blessing to those who "keep the words of this prophecy." John finishes this segment still in his vision as he continues to interact with the angel and then is told to openly share this prophecy, not to seal it up, for it is intended to be written and sent to the seven churches in Asia Minor. The angel then comforts John, assuring him that God will preserve this message no matter how crazy it might seem to some. If people are going to follow God, they will. If they aren't then they won't. The job of all Christians is to share the Word, to plant seeds, and to be at the work of Christ. If we are labeled heretics or crazy, then let it be so. The angel seems to be reassuring John that this vision is God's plan for the church. Finding Christ here seems to be a reinforcement of this vision and of the Great Commission; that after sixty years of persecution, God's plan still is the church's mission, and we can still find Christ in that purpose.

---

1. What is your understanding of the river of life, the tree of life, and God's throne?
2. What do the 12 fruits that come monthly mean?
3. What was John thinking at the end of this vision? Did he have apprehensions?
4. What insights did you gain from this session's word studies?
5. Share your thoughts and questions from this week's study.

Assigned for next session: (1) Read Revelation chapter 22 daily; (2) Journal and record your thoughts and questions; (3) Complete session #48 for next class.

Notes

Notes

SESSION 48

THE BOOK OF REVELATION

REVELATION 22:12-21 (KJV)

JESUS TESTIFIES TO THE CHURCHES

(12) And, behold, I come quickly; and my **reward** is with me, to give every man according as his work shall be. **(13)** I am Alpha and Omega, the beginning and the end, the first and the last. **(14)** Blessed are they that do his commandments, that they may have right to the tree of life, and may enter in through the gates into the city. **(15)** For without are dogs, and sorcerers, and whoremongers, and murderers, and idolaters, and whosoever loveth and maketh a lie. **(16)** I Jesus have sent mine angel to testify unto you these things in the churches. I am the root and the offspring of David, and the bright and morning star. **(17)** And the Spirit and the bride say, Come. And let him that heareth say, Come. And let him that is athirst come. And whosoever will, let him take the water of life freely. **(18)** For I testify unto every man that heareth the words of the prophecy of this book, If any man shall add unto these things, God shall add unto him the plagues that are written in this book: **(19)** And if any man shall take away from the words of the book of this prophecy, God shall take away his part out of the book of life, and out of the holy city, and from the things which are written in this book. **(20)** He which testifieth these things saith, Surely I come quickly. Amen. Even so, come, Lord Jesus. **(21)** The grace of our Lord Jesus Christ be with you all. Amen.

---

reward (GRK: μισθός/ mis-thos'): Wages; pay or salary; recompense or punishment; appropriate compensation; a particular decision-action; the result of toils and endeavors; (Jn 4:36/ 1 Cor. 9:18); divine recompense.

REFLECTIONS ON REVELATION

JESUS IS GOD

If there are some in the church who still doubt the deity of Christ or the authenticity of God's love, let them study Revelation. In this book, which was intentionally placed at the very end of God's Word, there is a clear message that Jesus means to present Himself as fully God and fully Man. He is the Alpha and Omega, the Root of the Offspring of David, and He is the only way to God. God's holy church has always been the entity that God chose to tell the story of salvation and to continue the ministry of the Great Commission given to all disciples of Christ at His ascension. All those who set out on their own without the covering of the church, which God chose to lead his children, are making a mistake. To truly enter into authority given by God you must be under the authority given by God. No one should ever resist the command to go to and be a part of God's holy church; it is where the work of God happens. Within these toils, both great and small, throughout church history, God's rewards will be given to those who serve. However, the greatest reward is deliverance from the sin nature that all persons are born with! The description of the great city we see here is only a dim picture of what is obviously an awe-inspiring place, a place of eternal life and blessing, and all who choose to reject salvation will not be allowed in this place. This is a clear message that, even though you cannot earn salvation through works, you must choose to allow salvation, by the power of the Holy Spirit, to transform you spiritually so that the Holy Spirit, God's Nature in you, produces works. While studying Revelation we are all reminded that now is not the time of rest, it is the time of work because redemption is so valuable (James 2:14-26; Rom. 4:1-8). Our status with Christ gives us the justification to lead others to the faith. Verse seventeen is written in the present verb tense, which is an invitation for all to receive Christ here and now. This is the work that is presented to the church, here and now, and on every day; to share the Kingdom with the lost. This vision from God ends with a warning to leave this message alone, to not add any other religious doctrines to it, and to not dismiss it or diminish its importance. Some argue that, in God's perfect plan, this message comes at the very end of the Bible in order to reinforce the message that the entirety of the Bible should be protected and kept from false doctrines. I think we can all agree with that if you see the inerrancy of the scriptures. Spend some time recruiting disciples and new groups to do this study; work for the faith and adopt the intentional purpose of God to bring the lost to salvation. That is where we find Crist in this study and in all aspects of life. As John finishes with a blessing, so I leave you. It has been an incredible journey! God bless you and God keep you, until we all see Him face to face. A. Pomerinke ⋌

---

1. What impact has the study of Revelation had on your life?
2. After a period of time, should you repeat this study?
3. What insights did you gain from this session's word study?
4. Share your thoughts and questions from this week's study.

Notes

Notes

About the Author

Arland Pomerinke has been a Christian speaker and evangelist for over thirty-seven years. He is a husband and father. His ministry throughout this time was affiliated to many Christian denominations, and he has worked to unite all Christians in the pursuit of discipleship for the common goal of fulfilling the Great Commission. A belief that all Christians literally have the same mission from God has been a call on this ministry. Thus, Arland has focused his ministry in bridging the perceived gap between churches of different doctrines and denominations to come together under one salvation and one mission.

He has a bachelor's degree in Religion and Christian Education, a master's degree in Clinical Social Work. He has been involved in clinical therapy and Christian counseling for many years and is committed to undertake the task of bringing the counseling field into awareness of the importance of spirituality in personal, emotional, and mental development.

Currently, Arland is a licensed mental health counselor and a designated crisis responder in a county detention center. He has served in church leadership in several denominations as a pastor, youth minister, and board member. He is a Christian author and evangelist who welcomes invitations to speak about faith, church growth, youth ministry, and the mission of the end times.

Look for Arland Pomerinke's next publication coming soon,
"The Sermon on the Mount, The Doctrine of Jesus Christ"
From Matthew chapters five, six and seven.

This sermon was delivered by Jesus and is an exposition on the Ten Commandments. It was intended by Jesus Christ to be His doctrine for the Church, and it remains the greatest sermon ever delivered, in one place, and at one time, by our Lord. It includes well-known teachings on Christian ethics and values, the dangers of pacifism, the Beatitudes, the call to be salt and light, turning the other cheek, the Lord's Prayer, the work of the Kingdom, morality, justice, and righteousness.

Printed in the United States
By Bookmasters